The Cookbook

Higgidy

FAMILY KITCHEN

new edition

The Cookbook

100 recipes for pies and more

CAMILLA STEPHENS

**MITCHELL
BEAZLEY**

CONTENTS

a note from Camilla, founder of **<u>HIGGIDY</u>**

To say I was born with a whisk in my hand might be a slight overstatement. But only just. Ever since I was very small I have loved to cook. What started off as an excuse to make a mess without getting into too much trouble with Mum soon turned into my favourite way to spend an afternoon. To be in the kitchen – mixing, chopping, stirring, simmering – was to be happy. And I soon learned that it was a brilliant way to make others happy, too.

Never in my wildest dreams did I imagine I would start a pie company – or even write a cookbook. But it's clear to me now that the journey I have taken owes everything to that childhood realisation: food brings joy.

Since then I've learned that pleasure, as vital as it is, is only part of the story. Food nurtures and comforts. It brings people together. It's for sharing and celebrating. Food, at its heart, is about family.

So in these pages you'll find no fancy restaurant dishes, no smears or foams or fiddly garnishes. Nor will you come across any low-carb, fat-free fare – as much as it has its place. This book is about feel-good family food: recipes that warm the heart and feed the soul. As a wise person once said: little reassures like a very good pie.

As a mum juggling family and work, I know how daunting it can be putting a meal on the table, coaxing children to try new foods and keeping cooking fun and interesting. So in this book you'll find plenty of simple suppers that can be made quickly after work or prepared ahead and popped in the oven just before serving.

There was a time, not too long ago, when I felt duty-bound to make everything from scratch. But I'm becoming more and more attracted to what I like to call 'crafty cooking'. These days I'll happily mix and match my own creations with good, shop-bought staples: some smoky grilled artichokes to sit alongside a homemade quiche, or a tub of top-notch ice cream to go with a carefully made pud. Scratch cooking can be immensely satisfying, but so can a spot of judicious corner cutting. What's more, and I'll whisper this, using ready-made puff pastry is absolutely fine.

about Camilla and <u>HIGGIDY</u>

In this latest edition, I've included 14 new recipes, all of which are very easy to put together. There's my Scandi Salmon Fish Pie Parcels, both quicker and lighter than a traditional fish pie. Not to mention my Raspberry Almond Pithivier, which is unabashed in its use of ready-made puff pastry, raspberry jam and marzipan. (It's not cheating; it's resourceful.)

For those of us with friends avoiding wheat, I've included several gluten-free recipes, including a fabulous Roasted Sweet Potato, Chorizo and Chard Quiche, and my recipe for Cranberry and Orange Gluten-free Mince Pies. Having to pass on a mince pie… that's just unthinkable.

And there are recipes for days when you have more time on your hands. I show how to use different types of pastry for quiches, tarts, baskets, vol-au-vents, tartlets – even a frying-pan pie. Traditional favourites such as Quiche Lorraine sit alongside more unusual creations, including a whole chapter of party pies, from a beautiful Wedding Pie to Mini Hot Dog Rolls, which can be made ahead and served straight from the oven. Some of these recipes take a little more thought and effort, but they bring immense joy – especially on a rainy Sunday afternoon.

Towards the back of the book, there is a whole section on pudding pies and sweet treats. These recipes underwent particularly thorough testing – purely for professional reasons, you understand. Then I share some handy ideas for side dishes and my top tips for pastry, along with some sneaky secrets I've learnt along the way.

If you enjoy cooking these dishes half as much as I enjoyed creating them, we should both be extremely happy. Remember, it's not about striving for perfection. The slightly burned edges of butter bean mash atop a Chicken and Ham Hock Pie, or the gooey undercooked middle of a Mud Pie Cookie – these are the best bits. So, let's celebrate them in all their imperfect glory. After all, the best things in life are always a bit Higgidy.

Camilla Stephens began making pies in 2003, having trained as a cook at Leiths School of Food and Wine. She worked for a time as head of food development for Starbucks UK, but as Starbucks expanded, Camilla decided to follow her dreams and start her own food business. And so Higgidy was born.

At the time, shop-bought pies were unashamedly masculine, and Camilla saw an opportunity to add some life and colour to the category, with vibrant new recipes that appealed to women and families as well as men. So she took traditional dishes and gave them a fresh, exciting twist.

Since then Higgidy has evolved to make what they call 'feel-good family food': nourishing, homely, wholesome dishes to enjoy together – whether it's their gourmet pies, quiches, veggie rolls or frittatas.

Camilla's recipes have seen Higgidy become one of the fastest-growing food companies in the UK, with their creations now stocked in most of Britain's major supermarkets. She is married to James and they have two children, Kate and Jack, who also love to make a mess in the kitchen. This is her first cookbook.

a few **COOKING NOTES** to help you along the way

We recommend using free-range eggs, poultry and meat for all our recipes. And always let them come to room temperature before cooking.

Onions and garlic should be peeled, unless otherwise directed. Try not to be too brutal when cooking them; cook gently unless the recipe specifically directs a sizzling-hot flame.

If using ready-made stock, choose a good-quality one for the best results and most balanced flavour.

Where herbs are called for, we really do recommend using fresh. The dried ones in jars just aren't as vibrant.

For recipes which use citrus zest, it's best to use unwaxed fruit. But if you can't get hold of any, simply wash waxed fruit thoroughly in warm, soapy water – remembering to rinse before using.

1 teaspoon = 5ml; 1 tablespoon = 15ml. All spoon measures are level unless otherwise specified.

Oven temperatures are given in degrees Celsius, with the equivalents for fan-assisted and gas ovens, and you can find a conversion chart on page 222 if working with degrees Fahrenheit. But remember that ovens do vary, so use our timings as a guide and always keep an eye on your cooking. An oven thermometer is a great investment for pie-making and will soon earn its keep.

And finally, we'd recommend doing as much advance prep as you can and leaving the final bake or stage of assembly for when you're ready to eat. This keeps stress to a minimum and makes for a more enjoyable meal for you and your guests.

and a **QUICK NOTE** about tins, pie dishes and funnels

Each pie recipe shows the size of pie dish or tin that's needed for baking. In most cases we don't specify the exact material – it would be a little daft having to rush out and buy something specifically. However, if you're lucky enough to have a deep cupboard with all sorts of cooking pots and baking tins, here are some tips:

* Bake double-crust pies in metallic or enamel pie tins as they conduct the heat better than ceramic dishes.

* Deep ceramic dishes are good for pies that only have a pastry lid, but you may well need a pie funnel. This acts like a chimney, allowing steam to escape from the hot filling so that it doesn't bubble up through the pastry. A funnel also gives support to the lid, helping to stop it sagging or losing its shape. Place the funnel in the middle of the uncooked pie with its top poking up through the pastry. You can even buy fun, decorative funnels that add to the drama of your finished creation.

* For quiches and tarts, loose-bottomed tins are great. They give a lovely even bake and make it easy to remove the tin before showing off your work of art at the table.

* Sweet fruit pies and cobblers work best in shallower dishes or pie plates, allowing you to cut generous wedges, and making it more likely that the pastry at the centre of the dish gets cooked right through.

simple
SUPPERS

pea and parmesan
PARCELS

We're rather partial to peas at Higgidy – it might sound a bit childish, but we've been known to have little more for supper than a huge bowl of peas with a knob of melted butter and some sea salt. So in honour of this fondness we've devised a pastry parcel around the humble pea.

250g frozen petits pois
4 spring onions, finely chopped
50g blanched almonds, roughly chopped
1 medium egg, beaten
100g cream cheese
100g feta cheese, crumbled
50g Parmesan cheese, finely grated
6 sheets of filo pastry
75g butter, melted
About 30 fresh mint leaves
Sea salt flakes and freshly ground black pepper

1 Preheat the oven to 200°C/fan 180°C/gas mark 6. Put the petits pois, spring onions, almonds, beaten egg, cream cheese, feta and Parmesan into a big bowl and mix well. It's easiest to do this with your hands to make sure all the ingredients are thoroughly combined. Season well with salt and pepper.

2 Lay a sheet of filo on your work surface and brush it with melted butter. Place 10 whole mint leaves randomly on top and sandwich with a second sheet of filo. Brush again with melted butter. Cut your double-thickness filo in half, lengthways, to give you two oblongs.

3 Starting at one end of an oblong, spoon one-sixth of the filling mixture on to the filo towards a corner. Fold over the corner with the filling on it diagonally to form a triangle. Continue to fold in this way, retaining the triangle shape. Repeat with the second oblong.

4 Now repeat steps 2 and 3 with the next two sheets of filo and half the remaining filling, then with the last two sheets and the rest of the filling so that you have six triangles.

5 Place the triangles on a cold baking tray that's lined with non-stick baking paper. Brush with the remaining butter and sprinkle with sea salt flakes. Bake in the oven for 20 minutes or until golden and crisp.

sausage and bean **PIE**
with ciabatta crumbs

SERVES
4

EQUIPMENT
1 x 2.5–3-litre shallow ovenproof casserole pan

The secret to success with this recipe is the lovely spiced tomato sauce and the use of good-quality Toulouse sausages. It's quick to fling together and you can even use slightly stale bread. We bet this one becomes a family favourite.

1 quantity of Spiced Tomato Sauce (see page 203)
4 tbsp olive oil
8 good-quality Toulouse sausages
150g chorizo cooking sausage, sliced
1 x 400g tin of cannellini beans, drained and rinsed
1 small bunch of fresh flat-leaf parsley,
  leaves chopped
140g ciabatta bread, torn into pieces
Zest of 1 lemon, grated or peeled with a zester
Salt

1 Make the Spiced Tomato Sauce according to the method on page 203. Preheat the oven to 200°C/fan 180°C/gas mark 6.

2 Heat 2 tablespoons of olive oil in your casserole pan over a medium-high heat. Add the sausages and brown them all over, then add the chorizo and fry for a minute or two, or until starting to crisp at the edges. At this stage your sausages won't be fully cooked through, but that's okay. Add the beans, half the parsley and the tomato sauce.

3 Pulse the torn ciabatta in a food processor for just a few seconds, until it forms rough breadcrumbs. Stir in the remaining oil, half the remaining parsley, half the lemon zest and a little salt.

4 Pile the crumb mixture on top of the sausage mixture, spread out evenly and bake in the oven for 35–40 minutes or until the crust is golden and the sausages are cooked through. Cover with foil if it starts to brown too much. Once cooked, sprinkle with the remaining parsley and lemon zest and serve.

summery pizza **PIE**

SERVES
8

**Samphire is a sea vegetable that likes growing on mud flats –
one place we've found it is on the north Norfolk coast. It can
sometimes be found in fishmongers and supermarkets, when
in season. It has a crisp texture and tastes of the sea. It's good
cooked very simply, in butter; we've used it to top our summery
pizza pie. If you can't find it, asparagus is just as delicious.**

1 quantity of Savoury Croustade Pastry
   (see page 217)
A little plain flour, for dusting

FOR THE FILLING
A knob of butter
3 garlic cloves, roughly chopped
200g baby courgettes (approx. 6), cut into
   1.5cm slices on an angle
4 large spring onions, cut into 1.5cm slices
   on an angle
75g samphire, washed and any large pieces halved
   (or use asparagus spears instead)
1 medium egg
250g full-fat cream cheese
Zest of 1 lemon, grated or peeled with a zester
2 tbsp chopped fresh flat-leaf parsley
Salt and freshly ground black pepper

FOR THE TOPPING
1 ball of buffalo mozzarella, torn
A little beaten egg, for brushing
Finely grated zest of ½ a lemon

1 Make the croustade pastry according to the method on page 217 and
put it into the fridge to rest for 30 minutes.

2 Melt the butter in a large frying pan. When it's sizzling, throw in the garlic
and courgettes and fry over a high heat for 2 minutes. Add the spring
onions and samphire (or asparagus) and fry for a further 4 minutes or
until the veg is beginning to steam but hasn't lost its vibrant colour. Set
aside to cool.

3 Beat the egg in a medium bowl and then beat in the cream cheese
until fully incorporated. Season with black pepper. Add two-thirds of
the cooled vegetables, the lemon zest and chopped parsley and stir
to combine. Preheat the oven to 200°C/fan 180°C/gas mark 6.

4 On a lightly floured surface, roll out the pastry into a 30cm circle,
about 3mm thick. Transfer to a large baking sheet (the pastry may
hang over the sides). Spoon the creamy mixture on to the pastry,
leaving a border of about 5cm all the way round the edge. Sprinkle
over one-third of the torn mozzarella and a good grating of black
pepper (and a pinch of salt if using asparagus). Top with the remaining
vegetables and mozzarella. Turn up the excess pastry around the
edges of the filling.

5 Brush any exposed pastry with the beaten egg and bake for about
25 minutes or until the pastry is golden and crisp. Remove from the oven
and sprinkle with a little fresh lemon zest. Allow to sit for 5–10 minutes
before slicing into wedges.

scandi salmon fish
PIE PARCELS

Fish pie is one of the most comforting meals – succulent pieces of fish in a rich, creamy sauce topped with smooth, buttery mash. What could be more soothing than that? This is a quicker, lighter take on a classic fish pie, but it really delivers on flavour. If you're watching the calories, you could go easy on the sauce, but for me, it sets this dish off beautifully.

400g new potatoes
1 red onion
2 tbsp olive oil
1 tbsp finely chopped fresh dill leaves
1 tbsp capers
200g cooked beetroot wedges
4 skinless salmon fillets
1 lemon, halved, for squeezing
Salt and freshly ground black pepper

FOR THE SAUCE
150ml soured cream
100g good-quality mayonnaise
1 tsp caster sugar
2 tbsp finely chopped fresh dill leaves

1 Preheat oven to 200°C/fan 180°C/gas mark 6. Cut the potatoes in half or quarters depending on their size. Peel the red onion and cut into wedges. Scatter the potatoes and onion evenly in a shallow roasting tin, drizzle with the oil and season with salt and pepper. Give the tin a good shake to coat the vegetables in the oil, then roast in the oven for 20 minutes. Don't worry if they're not cooked through, they'll finish cooking when they go back in the oven later.

2 Remove the tin from the oven and sprinkle over the dill, capers and beetroot wedges.

3 Cut four roughly 30cm squares of non-stick baking paper. Place a salmon fillet in the middle of each square, top each with an equal amount of vegetables and squeeze lemon juice over each salmon fillet. Fold two opposite sides of each baking paper square over the ingredients to cover, then fold the edges of the other two sides under a couple of times to create a sealed parcel.

4 Place the parcels on a large baking tray and bake for 15–20 minutes until the salmon is just cooked.

5 While the salmon is cooking, make the sauce. Measure all the sauce ingredients into a bowl and stir well to combine or whizz together with a hand-held blender.

6 Crack open the parcels, dollop over the sauce and eat immediately.

TIP

These parcels can be prepared ahead up to the end of step 3, then cooked on a barbecue and served with a simple pickled cucumber salad for a glorious summer's supper.

spinach, paneer and
spiced chickpea <u>PIE</u>

SERVES
4–6

EQUIPMENT
1 x 2-litre shallow ovenproof casserole pan

2 tbsp olive oil
1 large or 2 small red onions, finely chopped
2 garlic cloves, finely chopped
1 tsp mustard seeds
1 tsp medium curry powder
1 tsp ground turmeric
½ tsp ground coriander
¼ tsp chilli powder
1 tsp sugar
1 tbsp plain flour
400g tin of chopped tomatoes
200ml coconut milk
150g drained tinned chickpeas
80g baby spinach leaves
225g paneer, cut into cubes
50g butter
6 sheets of filo pastry
Black onion seeds, for sprinkling (optional)
Salt and freshly ground black pepper

At Higgidy we're always thinking up new ideas for pies, and our favourites are launched as 'Special Guests'. Some of them prove so popular that they stay for good, such as this creation. Don't be put off by the long ingredients list: I've simplified the recipe by topping with shop-bought filo pastry, which makes this one of the easiest pies to put together.

1 Preheat the oven to 200°C/fan 180°C/gas mark 6. Heat the oil in your casserole pan, add the onion and fry for 4–5 minutes or until it's beginning to soften and caramelise. Add the garlic, all the spices and the sugar, lower the heat and cook for a further 2–3 minutes. I sometimes add a splash of water so that the spices don't catch on the pan.

2 Keeping the heat low, sprinkle over the flour and stir well to combine with the spices. Quickly add the chopped tomatoes and coconut milk, increase the heat and bring up to a gentle simmer. Add the chickpeas and spinach and bubble gently for 4–5 minutes. Remove from the heat, stir in the paneer and season generously with salt and pepper. Leave to cool slightly.

3 Melt the butter in small saucepan over a medium heat. Brush a sheet of filo with melted butter and lay over the top of the spinach, chickpea and paneer mixture. Brush the remaining sheets of filo with melted butter, loosely scrunch them up and place them on top of the first piece of filo. Brush any remaining butter over the top. Sprinkle with black onion seeds, if you like.

4 Bake the pie in the oven for 25–30 minutes or until the pastry is golden and the filling is piping hot. Serve immediately.

TIP

I make this for a midweek supper and serve it with a quick homemade raita of freshly chopped coriander, tomato, red onion and cucumber tossed in natural yoghurt, along with some mango chutney.

chicken and ham hock **PIE** with garlicky butter bean and kale mash

Not only is this pie quick to throw together, it's gluten free, too. If you don't have butter beans, you can use any tinned white beans such as cannellini or gigantes beans.

EQUIPMENT
1 x 2-litre ovenproof pie dish

FOR THE FILLING
2–3 tbsp chickpea flour
2 tsp mustard powder
1 tsp cayenne pepper
500g chicken thighs
2 tbsp olive oil
100g or 4 large banana shallots, quartered
350ml hot chicken stock
200g cooked ham hock, pulled or shredded
    into finger-length pieces
250g mascarpone
Salt and freshly ground black pepper

FOR THE MASH
1 tbsp olive oil
25g butter
2 garlic cloves, crushed
75g kale, shredded
2 x 400g tins of butter beans
Finely grated zest and juice of 1 lemon

1 Preheat the oven to 200°C/fan 180°C/gas mark 6. For the filling, mix together the chickpea flour, mustard powder and cayenne in a large bowl. Slice the chicken thighs into large bite-sized chunks, then toss in the chickpea flour mixture to coat.

2 Heat a tablespoon of the olive oil in a large, shallow casserole pan or a large frying pan over a medium heat, add the shallots and fry for 3–4 minutes or until they have just begun to caramelise. Lift out of the pan and set aside. Add a further tablespoon of oil to the pan and fry the chicken pieces over a high heat for 2–3 minutes, then turn over and fry for a further 2–3 minutes or until golden.

3 Lower the heat slightly, return the shallots to the pan, add the hot chicken stock and give the mixture a good stir. Reduce the heat to low and simmer, covered, for 6–7 minutes. You may need to stir the sauce halfway through to stop the mixture catching on the bottom of the pan. When the chicken mixture is done, remove the pan from the heat and stir in the ham and 100g of the mascarpone. Season with salt and pepper and tip into the ovenproof dish.

continued...

chicken and
ham hock **PIE**
continued...

4 To make the mash, heat the oil and butter in a non-stick frying pan over a medium heat until sizzling. Add the garlic, kale and 50ml water. Turn the heat to low, cover and cook for 8 minutes or until the kale has wilted and is tender. Meanwhile, drain the beans and rinse well under the tap. Using a fork or potato masher, squish the beans to a knobbly mush. Stir the beans into the kale and garlic mixture and add the remaining mascarpone and the lemon juice and zest, reserving a little zest for sprinkling. Season with salt and pepper.

5 Spoon the butter bean mash over the chicken mixture and bake in the oven for 25–30 minutes. Sprinkle over the remaining lemon zest and serve piping hot.

simple
fish **PIE**

This recipe goes down as happily with children as it does at a smart grown-up dinner – though you might want to leave out the wine and reduce the seasoning if making it for little ones. Coley is not quite as well known as some white fish but it's delicious and, just as important, sustainable too.

SERVES
6

EQUIPMENT
1 x 1.8-litre ovenproof pie dish

1kg floury potatoes, peeled and cut into
   rough chunks
60ml semi-skimmed milk
2 tbsp olive oil
1 medium onion, finely chopped
300ml white wine (or replace with hot fish
   or vegetable stock if cooking for children)
300ml double cream
125g Parmesan cheese, grated
A handful of fresh flat-leaf parsley, leaves
   roughly chopped
450g salmon fillet, skinned, boned and cut
   into chunks
250g coley fillet, skinned, boned and cut
   into chunks
100g frozen peas
Juice of 1 small lemon
60g mature Cheddar cheese, grated
Salt and freshly ground black pepper

1 First, make your mash. Cook the potatoes in boiling salted water for 12–14 minutes or until tender enough to be cut like soft butter. Drain well and return to the pan, then cover with a lid and shake well so that they break up a little. Mash with the milk and plenty of salt and pepper until there are no more lumps. Set aside to cool.

2 Preheat the oven to 200°C/fan 180°C/gas mark 6. Heat the olive oil in a large frying pan, add the onion and fry for about 10 minutes or until soft and just turning golden.

3 Pour over the wine (or stock) and allow it to bubble for 3–4 minutes or until the liquid has reduced by at least half. Pour in the cream and bring just to the boil, then remove from the heat and stir in the grated Parmesan and chopped parsley. Set aside and allow to cool slightly.

4 Pour the sauce into your ovenproof dish and shake to distribute evenly. Place the fish chunks on top, along with the frozen peas. Squeeze over the lemon juice and gently toss everything together. Spoon on the mash and sprinkle with the grated cheese, then put the dish on a baking sheet and bake in the oven for 35 minutes or until golden and bubbling.

a hearty higgidy
HOTPOT

SERVES
6

For stew and potato lovers, this hotpot is hard to beat. Meltingly tender lamb and veggies in a rich gravy, topped simply with sliced potatoes, make this a great one-pot pie.

EQUIPMENT

1 x 3-litre shallow, lidded ovenproof casserole pan

2 tbsp olive oil, plus a little extra for frying
2 tbsp plain flour
600g lamb leg or neck, cut into 2–3cm pieces
2 onions, sliced
350g carrots, peeled and cut into thick slices
2 leeks, sliced
330ml Guinness or stout
450ml lamb stock
100g pearl barley
2 fresh or dried bay leaves
A handful of fresh thyme and flat-leaf parsley, leaves chopped
300–400g waxy potatoes, left unpeeled and thinly sliced
40g butter
Salt and freshly ground black pepper

1 Preheat the oven to 190°C/fan 170°C/gas mark 5.

2 Heat the oil in your casserole pan over a high heat. Season the flour with a generous pinch of salt and pepper. Toss the lamb in the seasoned flour and brown it on all sides. You may find it easier to do this in two batches. Remove the meat with a slotted spoon on to a plate and set to one side.

3 Reduce the heat to medium, then add the onions to the pan with a splash more oil if needed and cook for 5 minutes, to soften. Add the carrots and leeks and put the browned lamb back into the casserole pan. Stir everything together. Pour over the Guinness (or stout) and stock, and stir in the pearl barley and herbs.

4 Cover the filling with a layer of potatoes, overlapping the slices. Break the butter into small knobs, dot all over the potatoes and season with salt and pepper.

5 Cover tightly with the lid and cook in the centre of the oven for 1 hour, then uncover and continue to bake for 35 minutes or until the potatoes are golden and the lamb is tender. Spoon into bowls and devour. We don't think it needs anything else, but if you fancy something green with it try the Petits Pois and Pancetta (see page 195).

chicken and chorizo with spiced paprika **CRUMBLE**

SERVES 4–6

EQUIPMENT
1 x 2-litre ovenproof pie dish

FOR THE FILLING

1 tbsp olive oil

100g chorizo cooking sausage, sliced into
  5mm rounds

2 red onions, roughly chopped

3 garlic cloves, finely chopped

250g floury potatoes, peeled and diced

2 tbsp plain flour

450ml hot chicken stock

150ml single cream

1 cooked chicken (approx. 1kg) from a deli counter,
  skin removed and flesh torn into large pieces

Grated zest of 1 lemon

2 tbsp lemon juice

75g young spinach leaves, roughly chopped

Salt and freshly ground black pepper

FOR THE CRUMBLE

75g plain flour

100g dried breadcrumbs

40g Parmesan cheese, freshly grated

1 tsp smoked paprika

75g butter, chilled and diced

This is a super-quick recipe. Chorizo complements the chicken with its strong, smoky flavour and adds some fantastic colour. We've topped it with a spiced crumble that soaks up some of the delicious juices and makes a fine alternative to a puff pastry lid.

1 Preheat the oven to 200°C/fan 180°C/gas mark 6.

2 Heat the olive oil in a large, deep-sided, heavy-based pan with a lid. Add the chorizo, onions and garlic and cook over a high heat for 4–5 minutes or until the onions begin to caramelise and the chorizo starts to release its oil.

3 Add the diced potatoes and cook for 2 minutes. Add the flour and stir to combine, then pour in the chicken stock and give the mixture a good stir. Reduce the heat to low and simmer, covered with the lid, for 20 minutes. You may need to stir the sauce after 10 minutes to stop the mixture catching on the bottom of the pan.

4 Remove from the heat and stir in the cream. Pour into a large bowl and add the chicken pieces. Mix to combine then stir in the lemon zest, lemon juice and chopped spinach. Season well with salt and pepper and set aside.

5 Now prepare the crumble. Place all the ingredients in a large bowl. Using your fingertips, rub in the butter until the mixture resembles breadcrumbs. (Or you can do this more quickly in a food processor.)

6 Spoon the chicken filling into your pie dish and sprinkle over the crumble. Bake in the oven for 30 minutes and serve piping hot!

feel-good chicken and mushroom <u>PIE</u>

SERVES 6

Lighter than your average pie, but no less restorative. There's heat from the chilli, umami from the soy sauce and heartiness from the beans – all hidden under a crisp filo top.

EQUIPMENT
1 x 2-litre ovenproof pie dish

FOR THE STOCK
1 small chicken (1.25kg)
1 celery stick, roughly chopped
1 carrot, peeled and roughly chopped
2 sprigs of fresh rosemary
1 bay leaf
6 peppercorns
1 tsp mustard seeds

FOR THE FILLING
30g butter, melted, plus a knob for frying
250g chestnut mushrooms, sliced
2 garlic cloves, crushed
1 red bird's-eye chilli, deseeded and finely chopped
4 spring onions, finely chopped
1 small bunch of fresh coriander, leaves roughly chopped
300g tinned beans (a mixture of borlotti and cannellini is good), drained and rinsed
2 tbsp cornflour
2 tbsp light soy sauce
3–4 sheets of filo pastry
Salt and freshly ground black pepper

1 Make the stock by putting the chicken into a large saucepan with the celery, carrot, rosemary, bay leaf and peppercorns. Cover with cold water. Bring to the boil, then reduce the heat and simmer gently for 1¼ hours, skimming off any scum that forms on top. Take the chicken out of the pan and leave to cool.

2 Strain the stock into a clean pan. Bring to the boil, add the mustard seeds and simmer until reduced to about 1 litre. You only need 600ml here, so measure it now (you can freeze the rest). When the chicken is cool enough to handle, remove the skin and cut the meat into bite-sized pieces. Set aside.

3 Melt a knob of butter in a large, deep frying pan over a medium heat. Add the mushrooms, season with salt and pepper, and fry until just browned. Add the garlic and chilli and fry for a further minute. Stir in the spring onions and coriander and remove from the heat. Mix in the beans and chicken pieces. Tip into your ovenproof dish.

4 Preheat the oven to 200°C/fan 180°C/gas mark 6. Mix the cornflour in a small bowl with 2–3 tablespoons of the stock. Stir until completely combined. Pour the rest of the stock into a pan, add the cornflour mixture and soy sauce, then bring to the boil and bubble for a minute or two until slightly thicker and glossy. Pour over the chicken and bean mixture.

5 Melt the 30g of butter in a small pan. Brush a filo sheet with the melted butter and lay it on top of your pie. Brush the other filo sheets with butter, loosely scrunch and place on top of the first layer. Brush any unbuttered bits and bake for 35 minutes or until the filo is golden and crisp, and the filling piping hot.

mince and tattie **PIES**

This recipe is great for children; they love each getting their very own filled tattie. However, if you don't have time to fill the individual skins, simply put the meat into a large ovenproof dish and top with the mash – same taste, different look.

MAKES
12

EQUIPMENT
1 x 3-litre ovenproof casserole pan

6 large baking potatoes
2 tbsp olive oil
500g lean minced beef
2 onions, diced
2 garlic cloves, finely chopped
1 carrot, peeled and diced
200g swede, peeled and diced
2 tbsp plain flour
2 tbsp tomato purée
1 tbsp Worcestershire sauce
500ml hot beef stock
30g butter
50g mature Cheddar cheese, grated
Salt and freshly ground black pepper (if feeding
    very small children you may want to leave out)

1 Preheat the oven to 200°C/fan 180°C/gas mark 6. Pierce the potatoes once or twice with a sharp knife, place on a baking tray and bake for approximately 1½ hours. If they are on the small side, check them a little sooner to see if they are ready.

2 Heat half the oil in your casserole pan over a high heat and add the beef. Fry until it begins to break down and become dark brown. Remove from the pan and set aside. Add the remaining oil to the pan with the onions and garlic and fry over a medium heat for a few minutes, then add the carrot and swede. Continue to cook for 4–5 minutes, until the veg is beginning to soften and take on a little colour.

3 Return the mince to the pan and sprinkle over the flour. Add the tomato purée, Worcestershire sauce and stock. Give it a good stir and add some salt and pepper. Cover with a lid and simmer over a low heat for 20–25 minutes. Set aside.

4 Remove the potatoes from the oven, leaving it turned on, and slice in half horizontally (be careful; they'll be hot!). Using a big spoon, scoop the insides of each potato into a large bowl, retaining the skins. Return the empty skins to the baking tray and pop back in the oven to dry out for 5–10 minutes. Add the butter to the potato in the bowl and mash well to remove the lumps. Season with salt and pepper and set aside.

5 Remove the potato skins from the oven and reduce the temperature to 180°C/fan 160°C/gas mark 4. Fill each potato skin with a good spoonful of mince and top with mashed potato. Sprinkle over a little grated cheese and put back into the oven for 30 minutes, then serve.

chicken pot **PIE**

EQUIPMENT
1 x 2-litre ovenproof pie dish;
heart-shaped pastry cutter

45g butter
35ml olive oil
4 large leeks, sliced into fat rounds
2 large shallots, finely diced (or an onion will do)
500g chicken meat (a mix of breast and thigh),
  chopped into rough chunks
300g good-quality cooked ham, roughly chopped
3 sprigs of fresh rosemary, leaves stripped and
  finely chopped
4 sprigs of fresh thyme, leaves stripped and
  finely chopped
2 tbsp plain flour, plus a little for dusting
300ml hot good-quality chicken stock
200ml single cream
150g mature Cheddar cheese, grated
1 rounded tbsp Dijon mustard
800g all-butter puff pastry
1 medium egg, beaten
Salt and freshly ground black pepper

A pot pie is a baked savoury pie completely encased in buttery flaky pastry. This one has become a firm favourite at Higgidy and is always a hit when we take our portable pie kitchen (yes, really) to the festivals in the summer. This recipe is a slightly simplified version of the Higgidy classic, but is no less delicious for that.

1 Preheat the oven to 200°C/fan 180°C/gas mark 6.

2 Heat 35g of the butter with the olive oil in a large, deep, heavy-based pan over a medium heat, add the leeks and shallots, stir well and cover. Lower the heat and cook for 7–8 minutes or until the vegetables are soft.

3 Add the chicken and increase the heat. Stir frequently for about 6 minutes or until the chicken is just cooked through. Remove from the heat and add the ham and herbs. Give it all a good stir, then add the flour and stir to coat.

4 Add the stock, stir well and return the pan to the heat. Bring to a gentle simmer and cook for 2–3 minutes, to thicken. Remove from the heat, add the cream, cheese and mustard and stir well. Taste your filling and season with a little salt and black pepper if needed. Leave to cool.

5 Using the remaining butter, lightly grease your ovenproof dish. On a lightly floured work surface, roll out two-thirds of the pastry (about 500g) to about 3mm thick and use it to line the dish, letting the pastry drape over the sides. Pile in the cooled filling.

continued...

chicken
pot **PIE**
continued...

6 Dust the work surface with more flour, then roll out the remaining pastry to about 1cm thick and cover the whole pie with it, allowing the pastry to come just over the edges. Trim away any excess and press the edges together with your fingers to seal, or use the back of a fork. If you've got time and are feeling confident, you can crimp the edges (see page 210). Generously glaze the top with beaten egg.

7 Scrunch up the pastry trimmings and roll them out to about 3mm thick. Cut out some heart shapes and decorate the top of the pie with them, glazing with more beaten egg.

8 Bake the pie on a baking sheet in the oven for 20 minutes, then lower the heat to 180°C/fan 160°C/gas mark 4 and bake for another 20 minutes or until the top is puffy and golden. Serve immediately with a big bowl of garden peas topped with fresh mint and a knob of butter.

roast chicken dinner in a PIE

SERVES 4–6

This pie transforms leftover chicken into a comforting supper. Please don't take the filling quantities too literally – it's about using up leftovers and not letting anything from your Sunday roast go to waste.

EQUIPMENT
1 x 1.5–1.8-litre ovenproof pie dish

Approx. 220g leftover roast chicken (a mix of breast and leg meat if possible), torn into pieces and skin removed
Approx. 430g mixed leftover roast vegetables (or see tip)
A little plain flour, for dusting
375g all-butter puff pastry
1 medium egg, beaten

FOR THE SAUCE
50g butter
50g plain flour
150ml white wine (or use extra chicken stock if feeding children)
350ml leftover gravy mixed with 150ml water, or 500ml good-quality chicken stock
A few sprigs of fresh thyme, leaves stripped
75ml double cream or crème fraîche
1 tsp Dijon mustard

FOR THE STUFFING BALLS
220g sausage meat (or 3 sausages)
3 rashers of rindless streaky bacon, finely chopped
30g fresh white breadcrumbs
A handful of fresh flat-leaf parsley, leaves chopped

1 To make the sauce, melt the butter in a pan over a medium heat, add the flour and stir to a smooth paste. Gradually add the wine, if using, stirring until smooth, then gradually add your gravy or stock. Bubble for a couple of minutes, then remove from the heat and add the thyme, cream and mustard. Stir well, taste and season. Set aside to cool.

2 For the stuffing balls, mix all the ingredients, shape into walnut-sized balls and chill in the fridge until needed.

3 Preheat the oven to 220°C/fan 200°C/gas mark 7. Toss together the leftover roast chicken and cooked vegetables (cut into similar-sized chunks) and tip into your pie dish. Pour over the sauce and stir together. Arrange the stuffing balls on top – you can push them into the mixture a bit but they should poke up to support the pastry.

4 On a lightly floured work surface, roll out the pastry to about 5mm thick. Brush the sides of the dish with beaten egg. Drape the pastry over the filling and trim any excess. Seal the edges well and cut a steam hole in the centre. Scrunch up your pastry trimmings and roll out to about 3mm thick, then cut out decorative shapes and place them on the pie. Brush all over with the remaining beaten egg.

5 Reduce the oven temperature to 200°C/fan 180°C/gas mark 6 and bake for 45 minutes or until the filling is piping hot. Cover with foil if the pastry is browning too quickly.

TIP

If roasting vegetables from scratch, use 160g carrots, 200g parsnips, 160g leeks and 2 large potatoes, cooked and chopped into chunks.

chinese spiced
beef **PIES**

EQUIPMENT
4–5 x 300ml ovenproof pie dishes or
1 x 1.2-litre pie dish

1 quantity of Savoury Shortcrust Pastry
(see page 212 or use ready-made pastry)
1 tbsp olive oil
1 red onion, diced
1 celery stick, diced
1 carrot, peeled and diced
500g minced beef
1 red pepper, deseeded and sliced
2 tsp Chinese five-spice
4cm piece of fresh root ginger, peeled and
finely chopped
2 large garlic cloves, finely chopped
2 red chillies, deseeded and finely chopped
1 x 400g tin of chopped tomatoes
240ml hot beef stock
3 tbsp soy sauce
1 tbsp brown sugar
1 small bunch of fresh coriander, leaves chopped
A little plain flour, for dusting
1 medium egg, beaten
1–2 tbsp sesame seeds
Salt and freshly ground black pepper

Here, beef mince is cooked with ginger, chilli, spices and
soy sauce for a really punchy flavour. The sesame seed lid
is a lovely finishing touch. These little pies are great served
with some wilted Asian green vegetables.

1 Unless using ready-made, start by making the shortcrust pastry
according to the method on page 212. Put it into the fridge to rest for
30 minutes before using.

2 Heat the oil in a large pan over a medium heat, add the onion, celery
and carrot and soften for 5 minutes. Add the beef, season with salt and
pepper, then turn up the heat and cook until nicely browned, breaking
up the mince with a wooden spoon. Add the red pepper, five-spice,
ginger, garlic and chillies, mix well and fry for a couple more minutes.

3 Add the tinned tomatoes, stock, soy sauce and sugar. Heat until gently
bubbling, then cover with a lid and simmer for 15 minutes. Stir, then
simmer for a further 15 minutes, uncovered, to allow the liquid to reduce.
Stir in the chopped coriander and spoon the filling into your pie dishes
or big dish. Set aside to cool completely.

4 Preheat the oven to 200°C/fan 180°C/gas mark 6. On a lightly floured
work surface, roll out the pastry to about 3mm thick and cut out lids
(or one large lid) a little larger than your dishes (or dish). Brush the edges
of each pie dish with beaten egg, lay the pastry lid on top and seal
the edges with your fingers. Brush all over with more beaten egg and
sprinkle with sesame seeds. Cut a small steam hole in the centre of
each lid.

5 Bake in the oven for 30–35 minutes for individual pies, or 45 minutes
for one big pie, or until the pastry is golden and crisp and the filling is
piping hot. Some gravy may seep up through the steam hole but this
is rather nice and makes the pies look inviting.

spicy tomato and lentil layer <u>PIE</u>

SERVES
8

This is a really tasty vegetarian recipe that can hold its own as a main dish, with layers of aubergine, tomatoey lentils and creamy ricotta cheese wrapped in a pastry crust. Don't worry about leftovers; this pie is delicious served cold the following day.

FOR THE WALNUTTY PASTRY

400g plain flour, plus a little for dusting
½ tsp salt
100g walnuts
60g Parmesan cheese, grated
100g butter, chilled and diced
2 medium eggs, beaten, plus a beaten egg
    for brushing
3 tbsp ice-cold water

FOR THE FILLING

½ quantity (about 450g) Spiced Tomato Sauce
    (see page 203)
250g Puy lentils (we like the Merchant Gourmet
    pouches), cooked and drained
1 large aubergine
Olive oil, for brushing
200g ricotta cheese
Salt and freshly ground black pepper

1 To make the pastry, pulse the flour, salt, walnuts and Parmesan in a food processor until the ingredients are evenly mixed and the walnuts are finely chopped. Add the butter and pulse again until the mixture resembles breadcrumbs. Add the beaten eggs and ice-cold water and pulse until the mixture just comes together to form a dough, adding a tiny bit more water if you think it's needed.

2 Tip out on to a lightly floured work surface and knead very briefly to bring the pastry together. Don't worry if it's a little crumbly. Divide into two balls, then flatten into discs, wrap in clingfilm and chill in the fridge for 30 minutes.

3 Meanwhile, if you haven't already made the Spiced Tomato Sauce, do so according to the method on page 203 and let it cool down. Stir in the lentils.

4 On a lightly floured work surface, roll out one half of the pastry to about 3mm thick and trim to a 25cm square. Then roll out the other half in the same way, trimming it to a 30cm square. Put a piece of non-stick baking paper between the layers and return the pastry to the fridge to chill for a further 30 minutes. Don't be tempted to skip this step – it will help prevent any shrinkage in the oven.

continued...

spicy tomato and lentil layer **PIE**
continued...

5 Cut the aubergine into 5mm slices and brush each one with oil. Fry in a large frying pan over a medium heat until beginning to char and soften. Set aside.

6 Preheat the oven to 200°C/fan 180°C/gas mark 6. Remove your pastry from the fridge and place the smaller piece on a large non-stick baking sheet. Spread the tomato and lentil mixture over it, leaving a 2cm border all the way around. Top with the charred aubergine slices, keeping them away from the edges. Dollop the ricotta over the top, avoiding the edges again, then season generously with salt and pepper.

7 Brush the exposed edges of the base with beaten egg and place the second piece of pastry over the filling, allowing it to droop over the sides. Using the back of a fork, press the pastry edges together to seal. Decorate with pastry shapes if you like. Brush the whole thing with beaten egg and bake on the middle shelf of the oven for 40 minutes or until golden brown.

spiced lamb
babotie PIE

EQUIPMENT
1 x 2.5-litre lidded ovenproof pie dish

A little butter, for greasing

4 tbsp olive oil

1kg minced lamb

2 onions, finely diced

3 garlic cloves, crushed

2–3 tbsp medium curry powder (a little less
   for children)

¼ tsp ground cinnamon

1 thick slice of slightly stale white bread, crusts
   removed, soaked in water for 2 minutes, then
   squeezed dry

3 tbsp tomato purée

Juice and finely grated zest of 1 lemon

3 tbsp fruity chutney

1 Bramley or Granny Smith apple, peeled, cored
   and diced

50g dried apricots, chopped

50g raisins

3 bay leaves (optional)

4 medium eggs, lightly beaten

200ml thick natural Greek yoghurt

150ml whole milk

150ml single cream

30g flaked almonds

Salt and freshly ground black pepper

**This South African dish looks a lot like moussaka and has
a great combination of spiciness and sweetness. Despite
the long ingredients list, it's really easy to make and can be
prepared in advance. Serve with a pile of crispy poppadums
or doughy naans, a yoghurty salad of cucumber, mint and
garlic, and some fruity chutneys (mango is good) and pickles.**

1 Preheat the oven to 160°C/fan 140°C/gas mark 3 and butter the pie
dish. Heat 2 tablespoons of oil in a large pan over a high heat, add the
minced lamb and cook until evenly brown in colour, stirring all the time.
Scoop the mince and any cooking liquor out of the pan and set aside.

2 Heat the remaining oil in the pan, add the onions and cook them
on a medium heat for about 8–10 minutes or until soft. Add the garlic,
curry powder and cinnamon, and cook for 1–2 minutes. Return the
meat to the pan and stir in the bread, tomato purée, lemon juice and
zest, chutney, apple, chopped apricots and raisins. Add 200ml water
and simmer for 10 minutes. Season generously with salt and pepper.

3 Transfer the mixture to your buttered pie dish. Scatter over the bay
leaves, if using. Cover tightly with the lid and bake in the oven for 1 hour.

4 Remove from the oven, uncover and remove the bay leaves. If you
find residual fat has risen to the surface during cooking, use kitchen
paper to soak it up.

5 Increase the oven heat to 190°C/fan 170°C/gas mark 5. Mix the eggs,
yoghurt, milk and cream with a good pinch of salt and pepper. Pour over
the meat, then scatter with the almonds. Bake for 15 minutes or until the
top is bubbling and golden brown.

TIP

You can prepare this dish ahead to the end
of step 4, but you will need to reheat the meat
(covered) so that it's piping hot before adding
the creamy topping in step 5.

chilli beef **PIE** with spicy potato wedges

SERVES
6

This is one of those recipes that cheers the soul. It's pure comfort food, and perfect for a TV supper.

EQUIPMENT
1 x 3-litre lidded ovenproof casserole pan

FOR THE STEW

2 tsp cumin seeds

1–1½ tsp dried chilli flakes (depends on how hot you like it!)

1 tsp ground cinnamon

2 tsp dried oregano

750g braising beef, cut into 4cm pieces, excess fat removed

3 tbsp olive oil

2 onions, finely chopped

3 garlic cloves, finely chopped

1 small bunch of fresh coriander, leaves and stalks separated and chopped, plus more leaves to serve

2 green chillies, deseeded and diced

2 tbsp tomato purée

200ml red wine (or replace with extra beef stock if feeding children)

1 x 400g tin of chopped tomatoes

2 tbsp black treacle

200ml hot beef stock

1 large red pepper, deseeded and diced

1 x 400g tin of black beans, drained and rinsed

Salt and freshly ground black pepper

Fresh Red Salsa (see page 199), to serve

FOR THE WEDGES

4 large baking potatoes

2 tbsp olive oil

A good pinch of smoked paprika

A generous handful of grated mature Cheddar cheese

1 Preheat the oven to 180°C/fan 160°C/gas mark 4.

2 Grind the cumin seeds and chilli flakes together with a pestle and mortar, then tip into a large bowl and stir in the cinnamon, oregano and 1 teaspoon of salt. Add the beef and toss to completely coat.

3 Heat a tablespoon of the olive oil in your casserole pan over a medium heat and brown the spiced beef all over in batches, adding more oil if needed. Be careful, because the spices will become bitter if burned. Put the browned beef into a large bowl. Pour a little water into the empty pan, scrape the bottom with a wooden spoon to loosen the spices, then pour this over the beef.

4 In the same pan, heat the remaining oil over a medium heat, then gently fry the onions, garlic, chopped coriander stalks (reserve the chopped leaves) and chillies for 5 minutes or until soft. Add the tomato purée, wine, tinned tomatoes, treacle and stock and stir over a medium heat for a minute or two until well mixed. Add the beef and bring to the boil. As soon as the stew is bubbling, remove from the heat, cover tightly with the lid and cook in the oven for 2 hours.

5 Add the diced pepper and black beans to the pan, give it a good stir, season well with salt and pepper, then put the lid back on and return to the oven for another 20 minutes. Remove, taste to check the seasoning, and stir in the chopped coriander leaves. Set aside with the lid on tightly.

continued...

chilli beef **PIE** with spicy potato wedges
continued...

6 Increase the oven to 200°C/fan 180°C/gas mark 6. Cut the potatoes into chunky wedges and cook in a large pan of boiling water for 8 minutes or until just tender. Drain really well, then tip out on to a shallow roasting tin and drizzle with the oil. Sprinkle over the paprika and some salt and bake in the oven for 30 minutes or until crisp and golden. Preheat the grill to medium-high.

7 Now return to your stew, making sure it's still hot – give it a quick blast on the hob if necessary. Then scatter the potato wedges over it, top with the grated cheese and pop the dish under the grill, watching until the cheese is melted and bubbling. Garnish with fresh coriander leaves and serve with Fresh Red Salsa (see page 199), soured cream and guacamole on the side.

no-nonsense
steak and ale <u>PIE</u>

**SERVES
6**

As much as I love cooking with wine, there's something about this combination of steak and ale that's hard to beat. And while this might not be the quickest pie to make, it's certainly one of the simplest.

EQUIPMENT
**1 x 3-litre lidded ovenproof casserole pan;
1 x 1.8–2-litre ovenproof pie dish, about 5cm deep**

600g braising beef, cut into bite-sized chunks and
    excess fat removed
2 tbsp plain flour
250g small chestnut mushrooms, thickly sliced
3 garlic cloves, roughly chopped
2 onions, sliced
2 carrots, peeled, halved lengthways and cut into
    2–3cm crescents
2 celery sticks, cut into 2–3cm crescents
300ml brown ale
400ml hot beef stock
3 sprigs of fresh thyme, leaves stripped
1 tsp English mustard
Salt and freshly ground black pepper

FOR THE PASTRY
A little plain flour, for dusting
375g all-butter puff pastry
1 medium egg, lightly beaten

1 Preheat the oven to 180°C/fan 160°C/gas mark 4. Put the braising beef in the casserole pan and sprinkle in the flour. Give it all a good stir, until the flour disappears.

2 Add the mushrooms, garlic, onions, carrots, celery, ale, stock, thyme and mustard. Stir until everything is evenly mixed and season well with salt and pepper. Pop the lid on tightly, and put the stew in the oven for 3 hours, stirring occasionally so it doesn't catch at the bottom.

3 Check the stew a couple of times while it's cooking – you want this to cook slowly, with very little visible 'action' in the pan, just a murmur of bubbles on the surface. If it's bubbling too quickly, reduce the oven temperature. If the level of the liquid is low, add some water and give it a good stir. When ready, remove the stew from the oven and allow to cool completely. Transfer to your pie dish.

4 Turn up the oven to 200°C/fan 180°C/gas mark 6. On a lightly floured work surface, roll out the pastry to a disc just slightly larger than your pie dish, about 3mm thick. Brush the edges of your dish with beaten egg and lay the pastry on top like a tablecloth. Pinch the edges so they stick to the dish and trim off any excess pastry.

5 Cut a hole in the centre for steam to escape and brush the whole pie with beaten egg. Bake in the oven for 35–40 minutes or until the top is crusty and golden brown and the stew is bubbling down below.

giant gruyère and ham SANDWICH

SERVES
6–8

Ham and cheese is always a winning combination. This recipe is great for using up any leftover ends of cheese lurking at the back of the fridge, or bits of gammon from a Sunday joint. If feeding children, you can leave out the mustard.

A little plain flour, for dusting
500g all-butter puff pastry
A little vegetable oil, for greasing
1 tbsp Dijon mustard
3 tbsp crème fraîche
350g good-quality cooked ham, sliced
200g Gruyère cheese, grated
1 medium egg and 1 egg yolk, beaten together
Parmesan cheese, grated, for sprinkling

1 On a lightly floured work surface, roll out 200g of the puff pastry into a rectangle measuring 25cm x 30cm, and about 3mm thick. Place on a lightly oiled baking sheet and put in the fridge to chill for 20 minutes.

2 Preheat the oven to 220°C/fan 200°C/gas mark 7. Remove the pastry from the fridge and place a second lightly oiled baking sheet directly on top, oiled side touching the pastry (this helps weigh down the pastry to make it crisp). Bake for 20 minutes, then remove from the oven and take off the top baking sheet. Lower the oven temperature to 200°C/fan 180°C/gas mark 6.

3 Mix together the Dijon mustard and crème fraîche and set aside. On a lightly floured work surface, roll out the remaining pastry into a rectangle about 2cm larger on all sides than your base. Spread half the mustard mixture evenly over the cooked pastry base, leaving a 1cm border all round. Top with a layer of ham, then all the Gruyère and finally another layer of ham. Spread over the remaining mustard mixture. Brush the border with beaten egg.

4 Now place your uncooked pastry rectangle on top, press the edges firmly together and trim if necessary. You can make a pattern around the edges using a fork, or by crimping the pastry between your fingers and thumb (see page 210). Brush the whole thing with beaten egg and sprinkle generously with grated Parmesan.

5 Bake in the oven for 30 minutes or until puffy and golden brown. Set aside to cool for 15 minutes. Cut into 6–8 triangles and serve with a peppery green salad.

beef bourguignon
PIE

SERVES
6–8

EQUIPMENT
1 x 3-litre lidded ovenproof casserole pan;
1 x 2-litre ovenproof pie dish

4 tbsp olive oil
550g lean beef, e.g. chuck, blade or topside, cut
  into 3cm chunks
200g smoked bacon lardons
300g shallots, halved
1 large garlic clove, finely chopped
500g chestnut mushrooms, halved
3–4 sprigs of fresh thyme, leaves stripped and
  roughly chopped
2 heaped tbsp plain flour, plus a little for dusting
1 tbsp Bovril
250ml red wine
450ml good-quality hot beef stock
700g all-butter puff pastry
1 medium egg, beaten
Polenta, for sprinkling (optional)
Freshly ground black pepper
Garlicky Green Beans, to serve (see page 198)

This is one of our favourite pies, with its meltingly soft
pieces of beef, salty bacon lardons and rich red wine gravy.
You can forget the pastry lining if you wish and just go for
the crispy rough-puff lid, but we prefer it like this. It is worth
making the stew a day or two ahead, as it becomes even
more tasty.

1 Preheat the oven to 180°C/fan 160°C/gas mark 4. Heat 2 tablespoons
of the oil in the casserole pan over a high heat. Add half the beef and
cook until browned. Transfer to a large bowl, then repeat with the rest
of the beef.

2 Add another tablespoon of oil to the empty pan, then add the bacon
and cook over a high heat until just golden. Transfer to the bowl with
the beef. You may have some lovely burnt bits left on the bottom of
the pan – don't throw these away as they add flavour. Splash in some
water, scrape them up with a spatula or wooden spoon and add them
to the beef.

3 Heat the remaining tablespoon of oil in the pan, add the shallots,
garlic and mushrooms, and cook for 3–4 minutes over a medium heat
to get a little colour. Reduce the heat and return the meat to the pan.
Add the thyme and flour and stir in well. Add the Bovril, wine and stock,
stir well and bring to a very gentle simmer.

4 Cover tightly with the lid and place in the centre of the oven to cook for
2½ hours or until the meat is just tender. Slow and low is the secret here.
You're looking for the equivalent to a very low simmer – just a murmur
of bubbles, as we like to say. Check it every 40 minutes and if it looks
a little dry, top up with some water and give it a stir. To see if the meat
is tender, pinch a piece between your fingers or two spoons – it should
give really easily. Season with pepper (no salt) and leave to cool.

continued...

beef bourguignon
PIE
continued...

5 Turn up the oven to 220°C/fan 200°C/gas mark 7 and place a baking sheet on the middle shelf to preheat. On a lightly floured work surface, roll out two-thirds of the pastry to about 3mm thick and use it to line your pie dish, letting the excess pastry drape over the sides. Pile in the filling. Roll out the remaining pastry to about 5mm thick, to the shape of the pie, allowing enough excess to reach just over the edges. Place on the pie and trim away any excess.

6 Press the pastry edges together with your fingers to seal, or use the back of a fork. You can also crimp the edges (see page 210). Brush with beaten egg. Make two deep incisions on opposite sides of the pie – these will act as vents for steam to escape during baking.

7 Scrunch up your pastry trimmings and roll out to about 2mm thick, then cut out some pastry leaves and use them to decorate the top of the pie. Brush with more beaten egg. If you don't have time for this, you can sprinkle the top of the pie with polenta, which gives a really pretty texture.

8 Place the pie in the oven on the preheated baking sheet. Cook for 10 minutes, then lower the heat to 200°C/fan 180°C/gas mark 6 for another 30 minutes or until the top is puffy and golden. Serve with the Garlicky Green Beans on page 198.

lemony chicken **PIE** with quick soured cream pastry

SERVES
6

EQUIPMENT

1 x 2-litre pie dish or
6 x 300ml ovenproof pie dishes

1 quantity of Quick Soured Cream Pastry
  (see page 217)
A little plain flour, for dusting
1 medium egg, beaten
Dried oregano, for sprinkling

FOR THE STOCK

2 lemons
1 carrot, peeled
1 celery stick
A few black peppercorns
1kg boneless, skinless chicken thighs

FOR THE FILLING

75g unsalted butter
½ a fennel bulb, finely sliced
2 medium leeks, sliced
50g plain flour
125g semi-skimmed milk
100g frozen peas
Salt and freshly ground black pepper

If you're tired of the usual chicken recipes, try this one. Filled with lemon, fennel, leeks and a stack of herbs, it makes a fantastically fresh and wholesome lunch.

1 Make the quick soured cream pastry following the method on page 217 and put in the fridge to rest for 30 minutes.

2 To make the stock, remove the lemon peel with a vegetable peeler and squeeze out the juice from both lemons. Set the juice aside, and pop the peel into a large pan with the carrot, celery, peppercorns and chicken thighs. Top up with water until just covering the chicken and bring to the boil, then reduce the heat and simmer for about 20 minutes or until the chicken is cooked through.

3 Remove the chicken pieces from the pan using a slotted spoon and set aside to cool. Let the stock continue to bubble until only about 600ml remains, then strain off the vegetables and reserve the liquid.

4 Using your hands, tear the chicken into strips and set aside. Melt the butter in a large frying pan over a medium heat and fry the fennel and leeks for a few minutes until the leeks are beginning to wilt. Stir in the flour and cook for 2–3 minutes until bubbling, then stir in the reserved chicken stock and the milk. Bring to simmering point and cook for a couple of minutes to thicken the sauce. Stir in the reserved chicken, the peas and reserved lemon juice. Season well with salt and pepper, then set aside to cool.

continued...

lemony chicken PIE with
quick soured cream pastry
continued...

5 Remove the pastry from the fridge and set to one side while you spoon the filling mixture into your pie dish (or divide between the small ones). Preheat the oven to 200°C/fan 180°C/gas mark 6.

6 On a lightly floured surface, roll out the pastry to about 3mm thick and cut out a circle slightly larger than your dish (or six small circles for individual dishes). Brush the edges of the dish (or dishes) with beaten egg and lay the pastry on top. Using a sharp knife, trim the edges to remove any excess. Brush all over with more with egg and sprinkle with dried oregano.

7 Bake in the oven for 50 minutes or until the filling is piping hot and the pastry is golden. If making six little pies you may need to reduce the cooking time by 10 minutes.

stuffed portabella mushrooms with puff pastry <u>UMBRELLAS</u>

Mushrooms come in many shapes and sizes, and the portabella is one of the biggest and the best. This makes a lovely vegetarian brunch but is also a hit with meat-eaters.

6 large portabella mushrooms

A generous knob of butter

1 red onion, roughly chopped

1 fat garlic clove, finely chopped

1 sweet potato, peeled and coarsely grated
   (approx. 160g)

150g baby spinach

4 spring onions, finely sliced

1 heaped tbsp roughly chopped mint

65ml double cream

65g fresh breadcrumbs

Juice and grated zest of 1 small lemon

100g feta cheese, crumbled

A little plain flour, for dusting

320g ready-rolled all-butter puff pastry

1 medium egg, beaten

Salt and freshly ground black pepper

1 Carefully remove and roughly chop the stalks from your mushrooms. Lay the tops upside down on a baking tray ready to be filled.

2 Melt the butter in a large, heavy-based frying pan over a medium heat. Cook the red onion for a minute or so, then add the garlic, grated sweet potato and chopped mushroom stalks. Fry over a medium heat for 3 minutes, then stir in the spinach. Continue to fry for about 1 minute or until the spinach has just wilted. Remove from the heat and transfer to a bowl.

3 Once cooled slightly, stir in the spring onions, mint, cream, breadcrumbs, lemon zest and juice. Add the feta, season with salt and pepper, and give everything a good stir. Pile into your waiting mushrooms and pop them into the fridge.

4 Unroll your pastry on a lightly floured work surface and cut out rounds just a little larger than your mushrooms. Remove the mushrooms from the fridge and place a pastry lid on each one to completely cover the filling. Press down slightly to secure and brush with beaten egg. Scrunch up your pastry trimmings and roll out to about 2mm thick, then cut out decorative shapes (such as mini mushrooms) and place on top. Brush with more egg and chill for 30 minutes.

5 Preheat the oven to 200°C/fan 180°C/gas mark 6. Bake the mushrooms on the top shelf of the oven for 25 minutes or until the pastry lids are puffed and golden. Serve straight away.

spiced fish **PIES** with coconut crowns

SERVES
4
GENEROUSLY

This is a brilliant midweek, not-much-time-on-your-hands recipe. Don't be put off by the long ingredients list; the lion's share are likely already in your cupboard and, more importantly, the pies are absolutely delicious.

EQUIPMENT
4 x 500ml soup bowls

A little plain flour, for dusting
500g all-butter puff pastry
1 tbsp olive oil
1 large onion, finely chopped
1 tsp dried chilli flakes
1 tsp black mustard seeds
½ tsp ground turmeric
2 tsp cumin seeds
1 tsp ground coriander
600g tinned chopped tomatoes
1 red pepper, deseeded and sliced
1½ tbsp light muscovado or other soft brown sugar
Juice of 1 lemon
400ml hot vegetable stock
1 medium egg, beaten
50–60g dried coconut slices
150g basmati rice, rinsed
500g sustainable white fish fillets, such as hake
  or pollock, skinned, boned and cubed
200ml coconut milk
1 small bunch of fresh coriander, leaves chopped
Salt and freshly ground black pepper

1 On a lightly floured work surface, roll out the pastry to about 3mm thick. Cut out four rounds, each 1cm larger in diameter than your bowls, and put on a baking sheet lined with non-stick baking paper. Chill in the fridge for 20 minutes.

2 Meanwhile, heat the oil in a large saucepan over a low heat. Add the onion and soften for 5 minutes. Stir in the spices and cook, stirring, for a couple more minutes. Now tip in the chopped tomatoes, bring to a light bubble and stir in the red pepper, sugar, lemon juice and stock. Season well with salt and pepper, then bring to the boil and simmer for 10 minutes.

3 Preheat the oven to 200°C/fan 180°C/gas mark 6. Brush your pastry rounds with beaten egg and top each one with some slices of coconut. Bake in the oven for 15 minutes or until well risen and golden.

4 To cook the basmati rice, place in a saucepan, cover with 300ml cold water and season with salt. Bring to the boil, then turn the heat to low, cover the pan with a lid and simmer for 10 minutes or until the water has been absorbed and the rice is tender.

5 Add the fish to the tomato sauce and continue to cook for 3 minutes. Stir in the coconut milk and the cooked rice and simmer for a final 4 minutes, to warm through. Check the seasoning, adjusting to taste, and stir in the chopped coriander. Spoon into warmed soup bowls and top each with a coconut pastry crown. Serve immediately.

party
PIES

salmon and wasabi **STACKS**

MAKES 20 STACKS

EQUIPMENT
4cm fluted pastry cutter

A little plain flour, for dusting
125g all-butter puff pastry
1 medium egg, beaten
1 tbsp sesame seeds
1 tsp wasabi paste (if you like it hot you can use more)
3 tbsp crème fraîche
125g smoked salmon
50g radishes (5–6 medium ones)
¼ of a cucumber (about a 5cm chunk)

Wasabi is a pale-green Japanese horseradish and lends a real punch to smoked salmon. Try out these pretty little stacks if you want to impress guests with something delicious and unusual.

1 On a lightly floured work surface, roll out the pastry to about 3mm thick. Brush the whole piece of pastry with beaten egg and sprinkle with the sesame seeds. Stamp out 20 circles, using the pastry cutter. Place on a baking sheet lined with non-stick baking paper and chill for 30 minutes.

2 Preheat the oven to 200°C/fan 180°C/gas mark 6. Bake the pastry rounds in the oven for 12 minutes or until risen and golden brown. Set aside to cool.

3 Meanwhile, mix the wasabi and crème fraîche together and set aside. Cut the smoked salmon into 3cm pieces and thinly slice the radishes. Deseed the cucumber and, using a potato peeler, cut it into thin strips (keep the skin on, as the dark green looks pretty in the finished stacks).

4 To assemble, split the baked pastry rounds horizontally in two. Spread a little of the wasabi cream on each base, add a piece of salmon, a slice of radish and a piece of cucumber. Finish each one with a puff pastry top. Secure with cocktail sticks if you like.

mini chorizo and chilli **TARTLETS**

MAKES
30–36
TARTLETS

EQUIPMENT
30–36 mini tartlet tins;
5cm fluted pastry cutter

125g plain flour, sifted, plus a little for dusting
30g Parmesan cheese, grated
50g butter, chilled and diced
2 medium eggs
1 tsp ice-cold water
75g chorizo cooking sausage, cut into 1cm pieces
60ml double cream
1 red chilli, deseeded and finely chopped
2 tbsp very finely snipped fresh chives
Salt and freshly ground black pepper

We love these mini tartlets of smoky chorizo, spicy red chilli and bright green chives. They're wonderful served with the Beetroot and Feta Baskets (see photo opposite and recipe on page 64).

1 To make the pastry, place the flour and cheese in a large bowl or a food processor, add the butter and rub in with your fingertips or pulse until the mixture resembles breadcrumbs. Beat an egg with the ice-cold water and add to the mixture. Mix in with a round-bladed knife or pulse until the crumbs just come together to form a dough, adding a little more water if needed. Gather into a ball, wrap in clingfilm and chill in the fridge for 30 minutes.

2 On a lightly floured work surface, roll out the pastry to about 2mm thick. Using the pastry cutter, stamp out 30–36 circles and line your mini tartlet tins with them. Prick the pastry cases with a fork and chill for another 30 minutes.

3 Preheat the oven to 200°C/fan 180°C/gas mark 6. Combine the remaining egg with the chorizo, cream, chilli and chives, giving everything a good mix. Season generously with salt and pepper.

4 Divide the mixture between the pastry cases. We find the easiest way is to spoon the chorizo chunks in first, then top up the little cases with the rest of the creamy egg mix.

5 Bake the tartlets in the oven for 15–20 minutes or until the pastry is golden and the filling has set. Allow to cool slightly, then remove from the tins and serve.

beetroot and feta **BASKETS**

MAKES
30
BASKETS

EQUIPMENT
1 mini muffin tray;
5cm fluted pastry cutter

8 slices of white bread, crusts removed
30g butter, melted, plus a generous knob
A pinch of ground cumin
A pinch of ground cinnamon
250g cooked beetroot, grated
15g soft brown sugar
1 tbsp red wine vinegar
75ml apple juice
30g feta cheese, crumbled
A few sprigs of fresh thyme, leaves stripped

These tiny tarts are packed with flavour. The contrast of the intense purple-pink beetroot and the creamy white feta is visually stunning (see the photo on page 62), but it's the sweet and salty combo that really makes these a winner. They are easy to put together, too, because they don't require a pastry base – just simple sliced bread.

1 Preheat the oven to 200°C/fan 180°C/gas mark 6.

2 Using a rolling pin, flatten the bread slices to about 2mm thick and stamp out 5cm circles with the pastry cutter. Brush one side with melted butter and push each circle into a hole in your mini muffin tray, buttered side down. Bake in the oven for 10 minutes or until just golden.

3 Melt the knob of butter over a medium heat in a heavy-based pan. Add the spices and fry for 30 seconds, then add the grated beetroot, sugar, vinegar and apple juice and stir until everything is combined. Allow to cook for 6–8 minutes or until the liquid has dissolved and the beetroot has begun to look sticky and sweet.

4 Let the beetroot mixture cool slightly, then divide between the waiting bread baskets. Sprinkle each one with feta and a few thyme leaves.

giant tomato and parmesan **TWISTS**

You can make these in any size or shape, but giant twists do look impressive. They are a good way to use up leftover puff pastry, and not much can go wrong (especially if you use ready-made puff pastry). This recipe is a posh take on cheese and tomato, but you could substitute pesto (see page 202) for the tomato paste. Warm from the oven, these are hard to resist.

A little plain flour, for dusting

320g ready-rolled all-butter puff pastry (or any trimmings you have saved)

1 tbsp sun-dried tomato paste

1–2 tbsp chopped fresh flat-leaf parsley

1 medium egg, beaten

20g Parmesan cheese, finely grated, plus a little more for sprinkling

Freshly ground black pepper

1 Preheat the oven to 220°C/fan 200°C/gas mark 7.

2 On a lightly floured work surface, roll out the pastry into a rectangle approximately 30cm x 35cm and 1–2mm thick. Spread the sun-dried tomato paste evenly over the pastry and sprinkle with most of the chopped parsley.

3 Enclose the filling by folding the pastry in half from the longest side, creating a smaller rectangle. Roll out the filled pastry again (don't worry if some paste oozes out, it will all correct itself in the oven) into a rectangle approximately 30cm x 35cm.

4 Brush with beaten egg, then sprinkle over the Parmesan, scatter over the remaining parsley and add a generous grinding of black pepper. Cut the rectangle widthways into strips 2–3cm wide and add another sprinkling of Parmesan. Twist each strip three or four times.

5 Place on a baking sheet lined with non-stick baking paper, and brush again with beaten egg. Bake for 8–10 minutes or until golden brown. Allow to cool slightly before removing from the baking paper.

TIP

If using fresh pastry you can freeze the twists at the end of step 4. When you come to cook them, preheat the oven as directed, pop them straight from the freezer onto a lined baking sheet and bake for approximately 15–20 minutes.

mini hot dog **ROLLS**

Sausage rolls have the stood the test of time in the world of party nibbles, despite being sadly devalued by mass production. Even so, cheap ones sell by the million. Try our recipe and you won't look back. The photo also shows Mini Three-cheese Rolls – find the recipe overleaf.

450g free-range pork sausages or sausage meat
2 tbsp roughly chopped fresh flat-leaf parsley
1 medium egg, beaten, plus a little more
  for brushing
50g fresh breadcrumbs
1–2 tbsp olive oil
3 medium onions, finely sliced
A little plain flour, for dusting
500g all-butter puff pastry
Approx. 5 tbsp tomato ketchup
Salt and freshly ground black pepper

1 Preheat the oven to 200°C/fan 180°C/gas mark 6. Using a sharp knife, cut a slit down the length of each sausage (unless using sausage meat) and gently remove and discard the skin. Place the meat in a large bowl, mix in the parsley, egg and breadcrumbs, then season with salt and pepper and set aside.

2 Heat the olive oil in a frying pan over a medium heat. Add the sliced onions and fry for 5–8 minutes or until they have softened and begun to caramelise. Set aside to cool slightly.

3 On a lightly floured work surface, roll out the pastry to a 36cm square. Cut the square into three long strips, each 12cm wide. Spread or carefully squirt a little ketchup down the centre of each strip and top with your fried onions.

4 Divide the sausage meat filling into three portions and shape each into a roll the approximate length of your pastry strips. Place a roll along the centre of each strip, on top of the onions. Brush beaten egg along either side of the filling, then fold the pastry over and seal as carefully as possible. Turn the roll over so the seal is underneath. This prevents the roll opening up while cooking.

5 Brush each long roll with beaten egg. Dip a sharp knife in some flour and cut each roll into eight bite-sized pieces, to make 24 small rolls in total.

6 Place on baking sheets lined with non-stick baking paper and bake on the top shelf of the oven for 25–30 minutes until golden. Leave to cool on a wire rack before serving.

TIP

You can prepare these up to the end of step 5 and then wrap in clingfilm and freeze for up to 6 weeks. When ready to cook, simply allow them to 'come to' for an hour at room temperature, then brush with beaten egg, cut and bake for 25 minutes at the temperature given in the recipe.

mini three-cheese
<u>ROLLS</u>

MAKES
24
ROLLS

It's the mixture of three cheeses and scattering of pretty seeds that gives these little rolls the edge (see the photo on page 67). They're perfect party food – ridiculously tasty but still very affordable, and it's easy to make a big batch in advance.

2 tsp butter

1 tbsp olive oil

2 medium onions, finely diced

2 tbsp double cream

2 tbsp Dijon mustard

4 tbsp finely chopped fresh herbs (such as a mixture of flat-leaf parsley and chives)

1 medium egg, beaten, plus a little more for brushing

100g mature Cheddar cheese, finely grated

50g Parmesan cheese, finely grated

75g Cheshire or feta cheese, crumbled

100g fresh white breadcrumbs (you can make these from stale bread)

A little plain flour, for dusting

500g all-butter puff pastry

Black onion seeds and mustard seeds, for sprinkling

1 Preheat the oven to 200°C/fan 180°C/gas mark 6.

2 Heat the butter and oil in a pan over a low heat. Add the onions and stir until completely coated in the buttery mixture. Lower the heat, cover with a lid and cook for about 10 minutes or until the onions are soft and golden. Turn off the heat and add the cream, mustard and herbs.

3 Mix the beaten egg, cheeses and breadcrumbs in a large bowl until evenly combined, then add the onion mixture and give it all a good stir.

4 Now follow the recipe for Mini Hot Dog Rolls on page 66 from step 4 onwards (leaving out the ketchup for these cheesy ones), and sprinkle the rolls with onion seeds or mustard seeds before you bake them. This will help you tell the rolls apart if making both types.

mini mac and
cheese party PIES

MAKES
12–18
PIES

DEPENDING ON
YOUR MUFFIN
TRAY HOLE SIZE

EQUIPMENT
1 x non-stick mini muffin tray

100g dried macaroni or tiny pasta shapes
6 thin slices of prosciutto (optional – you'll need
  a little vegetable oil for greasing if omitting)
120g ready-made good-quality fresh cheese sauce
  (or make your own)
50g single cream
1 tbsp finely grated Parmesan cheese
A pinch of cayenne pepper
12g dried breadcrumbs
Salt and freshly ground black pepper

The trick to this recipe is to find a really good non-stick muffin tray – the heavier the tin, the better the quality. Serve the pies straight from the oven instead of a starter, or they make a brilliant snack or lunch-box filler for the kids.

1 Preheat oven to 180°C/fan 160°C/gas mark 4.

2 Bring a large saucepan of salted water to the boil over a high heat, add the pasta and cook according to the packet instructions until al dente. Drain the pasta, reserving 50ml of the cooking water.

3 While the pasta is cooking, cut or tear the prosciutto into strips and use to line each hole of the mini muffin tray, pressing them evenly into the base and up the sides. Don't worry if it's a bit messy and some of the prosciutto overlaps the top. If you are making these for vegetarians, make sure you brush each hole thoroughly with oil instead.

4 In a large bowl, mix the cheese sauce with the single cream, then stir in the cooked pasta. If you feel it's a little thick, add a spoonful or two of the reserved pasta cooking water. Season generously with pepper, then divide the mixture between the muffin holes.

5 Mix the Parmesan and cayenne with the breadcrumbs, then sprinkle on top of the cheesy pasta. Bake in the oven, on the middle shelf, for 15–17 minutes or until the edges of the mac and cheese pies are bubbling slightly and the tops are golden brown.

6 Allow to cool for 5 minutes then run a small knife around the perimeter of each muffin hole to loosen and remove the pies. Cool for a further 5 minutes before serving.

crispy asian
SALMON

This zingy Asian take on the classic salmon en croute makes for an impressive party piece.

3½ tbsp soy sauce

Juice and grated zest of 2 limes

1 tsp brown sugar

1 large garlic clove, crushed

1 x 700g piece of salmon tail fillet, skin removed, pin-boned (ask your fishmonger for the thicker end of the tail)

120g basmati rice, rinsed

1 red chilli, deseeded and finely chopped

2cm piece of fresh root ginger, peeled and finely chopped

2 tsp sesame oil

1 small bunch of fresh coriander, leaves chopped

4 spring onions, finely sliced

30g shelled pistachio nuts, roughly chopped

8 large sheets of filo pastry

60g butter, melted

Sesame seeds, for sprinkling

Salt

1 In a small bowl, mix together 2 tablespoons of soy sauce, the juice and zest of 1 lime, the brown sugar and garlic. Spoon this over the salmon in a large dish. Cover and leave to marinate in the fridge for 1 hour, turning over halfway.

2 Meanwhile, put the rice in a pan with 240ml water and a pinch of salt. Bring to the boil. Lower the heat and simmer for 5 minutes, then cover and continue to cook for another 5 minutes. Stir in the chilli, ginger, sesame oil, the juice and zest of the second lime and the remaining soy sauce. Transfer to a large bowl and allow to cool completely.

3 Stir the coriander, spring onions and pistachios into the cooled rice. Remove the salmon from the marinade and pat dry with kitchen paper. Preheat the oven to 200°C/fan 180°C/gas mark 6.

4 Working quickly, brush a piece of filo all over with melted butter. Place on a baking sheet, top with a second buttered layer of filo, then repeat with another two filo sheets, brushing as you go, to make a stack of four layers. Set aside, covered with a clean tea-towel (to prevent drying out). Do the same with your remaining four filo sheets – you'll need a second baking sheet.

5 Place the piece of salmon in the middle of one filo stack and spoon the rice mixture evenly over it. Lay the second stack of filo on top. Bring the top and bottom pastry edges together, fold up neatly and twist to seal. Brush the parcel with melted butter and sprinkle with sesame seeds.

6 Bake for 35–40 minutes or until crisp and golden and the salmon is just cooked through. Allow to rest for 20 minutes before cutting into thick slices.

giant garlicky mushroom **GALETTE**

Inspired by the vol-au-vent – and brimming with 'meaty' mushrooms sautéed with garlic and lemon – this puff pastry galette is guaranteed to impress. Place in the centre of the table, top with fresh rocket leaves, and let everybody dive in.

A little plain flour, for dusting

375g all-butter puff pastry

300g mixed mushrooms, such as chestnut, shiitake, oyster, enoki

30g unsalted butter

1–2 garlic cloves, depending on size, finely chopped

1 tsp finely chopped fresh thyme

Grated zest and juice of 1 small lemon

1 tsp Dijon mustard

200g ricotta cheese

1 medium egg, beaten

Salt and freshly ground black pepper

A handful of rocket, to garnish

1 On a lightly floured work surface, roll out the puff pastry into a large circle measuring 30cm in diameter and roughly 3mm thick. Place on a baking sheet lined with non-stick baking paper (the pastry may drape over the sides, that's fine) and chill in the fridge for 20 minutes.

2 Thickly slice the chestnut mushrooms and, if large, gently tear the shiitake and oyster mushrooms into smaller pieces. Melt the butter in a large non-stick frying pan, add the garlic and thyme and fry over a medium heat for 1 minute. Add the mushrooms and continue to fry for 2 minutes. Add the lemon juice and mustard, and stir to evenly coat the mushrooms. Season with salt and pepper. The mushrooms are going to get another cooking, so please don't feel you have to cook them through – they just need to 'see' the pan for now.

3 Preheat the oven to 220°C/fan 200°C/gas mark 7. Remove the pastry from the fridge and, using the back of a spoon or a palette knife, spread the ricotta over the pastry circle, leaving a border about 3cm wide. Pile the mushrooms on top of the ricotta and then fold in the pastry edges, pleating as you go. Brush the edges with beaten egg.

4 Bake the galette in the oven for 20 minutes or until the sides are puffed up and golden. Slide onto a large plate or board and scatter with the lemon zest and rocket. Serve immediately.

lemony lamb PIES
with feta mash

Lamb, olives and lemon are some of our favourite ingredients. Here we've crammed them into little Greek-inspired pies, with a delicious topping of cheesy, slightly salty feta mash.

EQUIPMENT

1 x 2.5–3-litre shallow lidded ovenproof casserole pan; 6 x 200ml ovenproof dishes or 1 x 1.5-litre ovenproof dish

1–2 tbsp plain flour
560g lamb leg, trimmed of excess fat and gristle and cut into cubes
3 tbsp olive oil
1 large red onion, finely sliced
1 large leek, sliced
1 large garlic clove, finely chopped
200ml white wine (replace with extra vegetable stock for children)
600ml hot vegetable stock
1 x 400g tin of haricot beans, drained and rinsed
50g pitted black olives
2 preserved lemons, quartered
½ a small bunch of fresh oregano, leaves chopped
½ a small bunch of fresh flat-leaf parsley, leaves chopped
Salt and freshly ground black pepper

FOR THE FETA MASH

750g King Edward potatoes, peeled and chopped into large pieces
A knob of butter
A splash of milk
1 tbsp roughly chopped fresh flat-leaf parsley
125g feta cheese, crumbled

1 Tip the flour into a large bowl and generously season with salt and pepper. Give it a good mix, then add the cubed lamb and toss to coat.

2 Heat half the oil in your casserole pan over a medium-high heat and fry the lamb in batches until brown all over. Set aside. Add the remaining oil to the pan and soften the onion and leek for 5 minutes. Stir in the garlic and continue to cook for 1 minute, then pour over the wine and allow to sizzle for a couple of minutes.

3 Return the lamb to the pan and pour over the stock. Bring to the boil, then cover with the lid and turn down the heat. Simmer gently for 1½ hours or until the lamb is lovely and tender. Add the beans, olives and preserved lemons and continue to cook, uncovered, for 15 minutes. Stir in the oregano and parsley, then spoon into the six ovenproof dishes or one large dish.

4 Preheat the oven to 200°C/fan 180°C/gas mark 6. For the feta mash, boil the potatoes in salted water until tender, drain well, then mash with the butter and milk. Add the parsley and two-thirds of the feta and give it a good stir.

5 Pile the mash on to your pies (or pie), top with the rest of the crumbled feta and bake for 20 minutes or until piping hot.

melt-in-the-middle pesto **CHICKEN**

SERVES 4

This lighter twist on the chicken Kiev is packed with just as much flavour. The pesto oozes out as a lovely surprise when you break through the crisp filo.

4 boneless, skinless chicken breasts
4 thin slices of Parma ham
16 sheets of filo pastry
40g butter, melted
Salt and freshly ground black pepper

FOR THE PESTO BUTTER
1 small bunch of fresh basil, leaves picked
25g pine nuts, toasted
1 large garlic clove, crushed
20g finely grated Parmesan cheese
100g unsalted butter, softened

1 First make the pesto butter. Pulse the basil leaves, pine nuts and garlic in the small bowl of a food processor until coarsely chopped (or chop by hand). Add the Parmesan and ¼ teaspoon of salt and pulse again.

2 Place the softened butter in a bowl and tip in the herby mixture. Mix thoroughly with a wooden spoon. Scrape out onto a sheet of clingfilm and roll into a log shape. Flatten the log, wrap in the clingfilm and chill in the fridge until solid.

3 Preheat the oven to 200°C/fan 180°C/gas mark 6. Place each chicken breast on a board and cover with a sheet of clingfilm. Using a rolling pin, bash the breasts until at least twice their original size. Season with salt and pepper.

4 Cut the pesto butter into four pieces and place a piece in the middle of each breast, then fold over the sides and ends to make neat parcels. Turn over so that the seal is underneath and wrap each one in a slice of Parma ham.

5 Lay a sheet of filo pastry on a board and brush all over with melted butter. Lay a second sheet on top, followed by a third and a fourth, brushing as you go. Place a chicken parcel in the centre and wrap it well in the filo, trimming away any pastry if you need to. Place on a baking sheet lined with non-stick baking paper and brush all over with melted butter. Repeat with the rest of the filo and chicken.

6 Bake the filo parcels in the oven for 30 minutes or until the chicken is cooked through, covering with foil if they start to brown too much. Serve warm, with a crisp green salad.

giant roasted red pepper and mushroom EN CROUTE

SERVES
8

Parcels are always exciting to receive – especially if they're edible! For this one we've wrapped some of our favourite vegetables in pastry with a layer of creamy ricotta cheese. It's big enough to feed lots of people, and makes a fabulous party piece.

6 large red peppers, cut in half and deseeded

A little plain flour, for dusting

750g all-butter puff pastry

A little vegetable oil, for greasing

75g butter

2 medium red onions, finely chopped

250g chestnut mushrooms, sliced

100ml double cream

250g ricotta cheese

3 heaped tbsp freshly grated Parmesan cheese

750g fresh spinach

1 tsp freshly grated nutmeg

1 medium egg and 1 egg yolk, beaten

Salt and freshly ground black pepper

1 Preheat the oven to 200°C/fan 180°C/gas mark 6. Roast the halved peppers in the hot oven for 35–45 minutes or until their skins have charred. Leave until cool enough to handle, then remove the skins, which should be easy to tear away from the flesh. Slice each pepper half lengthways into two strips and set aside to cool completely.

2 On a lightly floured work surface, roll out 250g of the pastry to a rectangle measuring 30cm x 15cm and about 5mm thick. Place on a lightly oiled baking sheet and top with a second lightly oiled baking sheet (this helps weigh down the pastry to make it lovely and crisp). Bake in the oven for 20 minutes, then take out, remove the top baking sheet and set aside.

3 Meanwhile, melt 50g of the butter in a frying pan over a medium heat and cook the onions until soft. Add the mushrooms and fry for about 7 minutes until the liquid has evaporated. Pour in the cream and allow to bubble until the mushrooms are just coated. Leave to cool, then stir in the ricotta and Parmesan. Season generously with black pepper and a little salt.

4 Melt the remaining butter in a very large saucepan over a medium heat. Add the spinach and cook until the leaves have wilted and any water has bubbled away. Drain and press out all remaining moisture: this is important as you don't want the parcel to be too wet. Roughly chop the spinach and season with salt, pepper and nutmeg.

5 To assemble, cover the cooked pastry base with half your roasted pepper strips. About 1cm in from the edge of the peppers, create a ring of chopped spinach and put the creamy mushroom mixture inside this spinach ring. Finally, top with the remaining red pepper strips. You will now have quite a high mound of vegetables.

6 Roll out the remaining pastry to a rectangle approximately 35cm x 20cm and 5mm thick. Drape this over the vegetables, tucking the edges underneath your cooked pastry base (you might need another pair of hands to help here). Brush all over with beaten egg. Scrunch up your pastry trimmings and roll out to about 2mm thick, then cut out shapes to decorate your parcel, sticking them down with beaten egg. Chill in the fridge for at least 20 minutes.

7 Preheat the oven again to 200°C/fan 180°C/gas mark 6. Brush the pastry with a little more beaten egg and bake in the oven for 35–40 minutes or until cooked through and golden on top. Allow to cool for about 45 minutes, then cut into thick slices to serve – it will still be lovely and warm but giving it this time to rest makes it easier to cut.

wonderful wedding **PIE**

FOR 1 MEDIUM PIE (MIDDLE TIER)

EQUIPMENT
1 x 20cm springform cake tin, 10cm deep

FOR THE HOT-WATER CRUST PASTRY
250g lard
1 tsp salt
750g plain flour, plus a little for dusting
1 egg, plus a beaten egg for glazing

FOR THE FILLING
500g lean pork shoulder, cut into 1cm cubes
400g sausage meat
150g smoked streaky bacon rashers, cut into
   5mm strips using kitchen scissors
1 small bunch of fresh thyme, leaves stripped
1 tsp freshly grated nutmeg
2 tbsp redcurrant jelly
1 medium egg, beaten
50g fresh breadcrumbs
2 duck breasts (about 300g), skin removed
   and meat cut into 5mm strips
200g semi-dried apricots
Salt and freshly ground black pepper

As far as we're concerned, this beats any wedding cake hands down. Crammed with rich duck, pork, apricots and garden herbs, it's worthy of any celebration. In fact, the main recipe, which is for the medium tier only, is equally good eaten at Christmas with lashings of chutney.

1 Start by making the pastry (hot-water crust pastry is quite a different technique from other types, so if you've not made it before, we suggest reading the whole method before you begin!) Pour 300ml water into a medium saucepan, add the lard and salt, and slowly bring to a simmer over a medium heat. Don't allow it to boil – you don't want any water to evaporate.

2 When the lard has melted, remove the pan from the heat and quickly add the flour. Using a wooden spoon, beat with gusto until the ingredients are amalgamated into a glossy paste. Crack in the egg and incorporate with more aggressive mixing. Turn out the dough on to a clean, lightly floured work surface and knead for a minute or two until smooth.

3 Reserve a third of the dough for the lid, shape into a disc, wrap in clingfilm and place in the fridge. On a lightly floured work surface, shape the remaining dough into a rough circle and place in the middle of your springform tin. Work it over the base and up the sides of the tin with your fingers until just peeping over the top. Put in the fridge to chill for 2 hours.

continued...

TIP
To make the small or large tiers or the whole three-tier wonder, turn to page 83. For special occasions, you can decorate your pie (or pies) with herbs, flowers, ribbons or even little bunches of grapes.

wonderful
wedding **PIE**
continued...

**TIP FOR
MAKING 3 TIERS**

If making all three tiers you will
need to cook them separately.
It's important to cook each pie
in the centre of the oven, which
allows the heat to circulate,
achieving a lovely even colour.

If you're keen to get all three
tiers the same shade of golden
brown, we suggest making the
top tier first, then mimicking
the colour on the two larger
tiers by increasing the cooking
time in 10-minute increments
until you are satisfied.

4 Preheat the oven to 190°C/fan 170°C/gas mark 5. Put the pork, sausage meat, bacon, thyme leaves, nutmeg, redcurrant jelly, beaten egg and 1 teaspoon of salt in a large bowl and mix thoroughly.

5 Sprinkle the breadcrumbs into the pastry case and put half the pork mixture into the bottom of the pie. Top with a layer of duck. Season with salt and pepper, then add a layer of apricots. Finally, top with the remaining pork mixture.

6 On a lightly floured work surface, roll the reserved pastry into a circle about 1cm wider in diameter than the top of the pie. Brush the top edges of the pie case with beaten egg and place the pastry lid on the surface of the filling. Crimp the edges to seal (see page 210). Make a 1cm hole in the centre of the pie so that steam can escape, and decorate with any leftover pastry. Now you've finished the hard bit!

7 Place the pie on a baking tray and bake for 30 minutes, then reduce the oven temperature to 160°C/fan 140°C/gas mark 3 and bake for a further 1½ hours or until the pastry has turned a deep golden brown. Take the pie out and allow it to cool for 15 minutes before removing from the tin.

8 To make the pie really glossy, you can brush with more beaten egg and put it back in the oven without the tin for another 20 minutes or until the pastry is lovely and golden, but this is optional if you don't have time. Before serving, allow the pie to rest overnight in the coolest room of the house. It can be kept in the fridge for up to 5 days if not required immediately (giving you time to make the other tiers if you wish).

Here are quantities for the top and bottom tiers, plus the total amounts needed for the whole three-tier pie (see also the tips opposite). For the medium-sized middle tier, see page 81.

	FOR THE SMALL (TOP) TIER	FOR THE LARGE (BOTTOM) TIER	FOR THE WHOLE WEDDING PIE!
Equipment:	1 x 15cm springform tin, 8cm deep	1 x 25cm springform tin, 10cm deep	3 x springform tins: 15cm (8cm deep), 20cm and 25cm (both 10cm deep)
For the hot-water crust pastry:			
Hot water	150ml	450ml	900ml
Lard	125g	375g	750g
Salt	½ tsp	1 tsp	2½ tsp
Plain flour, plus a little for dusting	375g	1.125kg	2.25kg
Eggs	1 yolk, plus 1 beaten egg for glazing	1 egg + 1 yolk, plus 1 beaten egg for glazing	3 eggs + 1 yolk, plus 2 beaten eggs for glazing
For the filling:			
Lean pork shoulder, cut into 1cm cubes	250g	750g	1.5kg
Sausage meat	200g	600g	1.2kg
Smoked streaky bacon rashers, cut into 5mm strips using kitchen scissors	75g	225g	450g
Fresh thyme, leaves stripped	Small bunch	1 x 30g bunch	Large bunch
Freshly grated nutmeg	½ tsp	1½ tsp	1 tbsp
Redcurrant jelly	1 tbsp	3 tbsp	6 tbsp
Eggs, beaten	1 yolk	1 egg + 1 yolk	2 eggs + 2 yolks
Salt	½ tsp	1½ tsp	1 tbsp
Fresh breadcrumbs	25g	75g	150g
Duck breasts, skin removed, meat cut into 5mm strips	1 (about 150g)	3 (about 550g)	6 (about 1kg)
Semi-dried apricots	100g	300g	600g
Follow method on p81–82 but use these cooking times: (see opposite for fan/gas marks)	15 mins (at 190°C), then 1 hour 20 mins (at 160°C)	30 mins (at 190°C), then 1 hour 40 mins (at 160°C)	See opposite and other columns for timings for each tier

christmas turkey **PIE**
with all the trimmings

SERVES
10

The beloved Christmas lunch shouldn't be exclusive to 25 December. Now you can indulge at any time of year! Chestnuts, turkey, bacon and sausage meat are encased in a gorgeous golden parcel, which can be eaten hot, warm or cold, and very easy to prepare ahead.

A little plain flour, for dusting
750g all-butter puff pastry
A little vegetable oil, for greasing

FOR THE APRICOT STUFFING
A knob of butter
1 medium onion, finely chopped
1 tsp fresh thyme leaves
1 tsp chopped fresh flat-leaf parsley
1 tsp chopped fresh sage
50g dried breadcrumbs
50g dried apricots, roughly chopped
250g good-quality sausage meat
Salt and freshly ground black pepper

FOR THE CHESTNUT AND BACON FILLING
3 knobs of butter
1 tbsp olive oil
1 medium onion, finely chopped
1 leek, finely chopped
1 celery stick, roughly chopped
1 tsp fresh thyme leaves
250g white mushrooms, thickly sliced
130g pancetta lardons
100g vacuum-packed cooked chestnuts, chopped
1 tbsp plain flour
100ml hot chicken stock
150ml single cream

TO ASSEMBLE
300g turkey escalopes
1 x 400g tin of apricot halves, drained
1 medium egg, beaten

1 Preheat the oven to 200°C/fan 180°C/gas mark 6.

2 On a lightly floured surface, roll out 250g of the pastry to a rectangle measuring 30cm x 15cm and about 3mm thick. Place on a lightly oiled baking sheet and top with a second baking sheet, also lightly oiled – this helps weigh down the pastry to make it nice and crisp. Bake for 20 minutes, then remove from the oven and set aside.

3 To make the apricot stuffing, melt the butter in a pan over a medium heat and add the onion. Stir for a minute, then cover with a lid and cook gently for about 5 minutes or until the onion is just soft. Add the herbs, breadcrumbs and apricots and stir well. Remove from the heat and leave to cool. Once completely cold, add the sausage meat, season with salt and pepper, and mix with your hands until evenly combined.

4 For the chestnut filling, melt a knob of butter with the oil in a frying pan over a low heat. Add the onion and leek, stir well, then cover with a lid and cook for 6–7 minutes or until the vegetables are just soft. Remove to a bowl and set aside. Pop another knob of butter into the pan, increase the heat and fry the celery, thyme and mushrooms for about 4 minutes or until the mushrooms are soft and golden. Add to the bowl with the onion and leek.

continued...

christmas turkey **PIE**
with all the trimmings
continued...

5 Melt the remaining knob of butter in the pan and fry the pancetta lardons for 4–5 minutes or until they have just turned golden brown. Tip in the cooked vegetables and chestnuts. Stir well, then add the flour and stir again. Over a medium heat, pour in the chicken stock and bring to the boil. Allow to bubble for 1 minute, then add the cream and immediately turn off the heat. Season with pepper and set aside to cool completely.

6 When ready to assemble, cover the cooked pastry base with the stuffing, leaving a 1cm border. Bash the turkey escalopes with a rolling pin until flattish and lay them over the stuffing. Place the apricot halves face down along the middle of the turkey, then carefully spoon the chestnut and bacon filling over the top. You will have quite a high mound by now!

7 Roll your remaining pastry to a rectangle approximately 35cm x 20cm and about 5mm thick, and drape it over the filling, tucking the edges underneath your cooked pastry base (you might need another pair of hands to help you here). Brush with the beaten egg. Scrunch up the pastry trimmings and roll out to about 2mm thick. Cut out stars or holly leaves and use to decorate your parcel, sticking them down with beaten egg. Chill in the fridge for at least 20 minutes.

8 Preheat the oven to 220°C/fan 200°C/gas mark 7. Brush the parcel with a little more beaten egg and bake for 20 minutes, then turn the oven down to 190°C/fan 170°C/gas mark 5 and bake for a final 30 minutes.

9 Allow to cool for about 45 minutes before slicing; it will still be lovely and warm but will cut more easily. Serve with cranberry sauce and roasted winter vegetables.

lamb shank
PIE

SERVES
6–8

EQUIPMENT
1 x 3-litre lidded ovenproof casserole pan;
1 x 2-litre ovenproof pie dish

2 tbsp vegetable oil
2 lamb shanks (approx. 400g each)
2 red onions, sliced
5 garlic cloves, chopped
2 tsp ground coriander
1 tsp dried chilli flakes
2 tsp ground cumin
1 tsp paprika
1 tbsp tomato purée
2 tbsp plain flour
4 large carrots, peeled and cut into 3cm chunks
1 x 400g tin of chickpeas, drained and rinsed
50g juicy raisins
500ml full-bodied red wine (or use extra lamb
   stock for children)
500ml hot lamb stock
1 medium egg, beaten
Salt and freshly ground black pepper

FOR THE TOPPING
A little plain flour, for dusting
350g all-butter puff pastry
1 medium egg, lightly beaten
1 tsp black onion seeds, for sprinkling

Here's a warming winter pie that makes a fabulous centrepiece for the table: lamb shanks cooked slowly with red wine, spices and sweet carrots, hidden beneath a fudgy, buttery puff pastry lid. The bones act as a pie funnel, which puts them to good use and makes the finished pie look very impressive.

1 Heat the oil in your casserole pan over a high heat and add the lamb shanks. Take care to turn each shank regularly until the meat is an even golden brown. Spend a good few minutes doing this; it is worth it for the extra flavour. Remove the shanks from the pan and set aside.

2 Add the chopped onions to the empty pan and fry over a medium heat for 3–4 minutes or until they begin to soften. Stir in the garlic, coriander, chilli flakes, cumin and paprika and continue to cook for about 30 seconds, then add the tomato purée.

3 Add the flour, carrots, chickpeas and raisins, then give everything a good stir and a healthy dose of salt and pepper. Pour over the red wine and hot stock and return the lamb shanks to the casserole pan. Cover with the lid and reduce the heat to its lowest setting. Cook, stirring occasionally, for 2½–3 hours or until the lamb is falling off the bone and the liquid has reduced. Set aside to cool.

4 Spoon out the lamb shanks on to a plate and transfer the saucy vegetables to your ovenproof pie dish. Using your hands or the back of a spoon, prise the meat from the lamb shanks, tear into bite-sized pieces and add to the dish. Arrange the naked bones sticking up in the centre of the dish (which will create a steam hole) and set aside to cool completely, preferably overnight in the fridge; the flavour only improves with a bit of sitting around.

continued...

lamb shank
PIE
continued...

5 When you are ready to bake the pie, preheat the oven to 200°C/fan 180°C/ gas mark 6. Roll out your pastry on a lightly floured work surface to about 5mm thick and cut out a lid a little larger than the top of your dish. Brush the edges of the dish with beaten egg and lay the pastry on top, using a knife to make holes for the bones to peek through. Gently press the pastry on to the edges of the dish.

6 Cut leaves from the pastry trimmings and use them to decorate the pie, sticking them on top with beaten egg. Brush the entire pie with more beaten egg, and sprinkle with black onion seeds. Bake in the oven for 40 minutes or until the pastry is golden and the gravy is bubbling up out of the steam holes.

dauphinoise potato
and onion **PIE**

EQUIPMENT
1 x 2.5-litre ovenproof pie dish

FOR THE PASTRY

400g plain flour, sifted, plus a little for dusting

A generous pinch of salt

200g butter, chilled and diced, plus a little more
    for greasing

Approx. 70ml ice-cold water

FOR THE POTATO FILLING

600ml double cream

200ml semi-skimmed milk

2–3 garlic cloves, crushed

1kg floury potatoes, peeled and cut into
    3–4mm slices

3 large white onions, halved and very thinly sliced
    into rings

100g Gruyère cheese, grated

Dried herbs such as thyme or oregano (optional)

1 medium egg, lightly beaten

Salt and freshly ground black pepper

Here we've taken the simple potato and onion pie, and
combined it with one of our favourite methods of cooking
potatoes. The result is a stunning pie that needs nothing
more with it than a crunchy salad, though a platter of cold
meats also sits very comfortably alongside.

1 Start by making your pastry: place the flour and salt in a large bowl
or a food processor, add the butter cubes and rub in with your fingertips
or pulse until the mixture resembles breadcrumbs. Mix in the ice-cold
water or pour slowly into the running processor until the pastry begins
to clump and come together. Tip on to a lightly floured work surface and
bring together using your hands. Shape into a disc, wrap in clingfilm and
chill for at least 20 minutes.

2 Meanwhile, bring your cream, milk, garlic and a generous pinch of
salt to simmering point in a medium saucepan. Simmer for a minute
or two, for the garlic to infuse, then remove the saucepan from the heat
and allow to cool completely.

3 Preheat the oven to 200°C/fan 180°C/gas mark 6 and put a baking
sheet in to heat up.

4 Grease the pie dish. On a lightly floured work surface, roll out your
pastry to about 3mm thick. You should have more than enough to lay
over the bottom and sides of your dish. Trim around the edges. Gather
up any leftover pastry, shape into a disc and set aside.

5 Layer up the sliced potato and onion rings to cover the pastry in
the bottom of the dish. Season with salt and pepper, and sprinkle over
a layer of Gruyère. If you like, add a scattering of dried herbs. Continue
to layer until all the potato and onion has been used. Slowly pour over
the garlicky cream mixture, allowing each addition to disappear before
adding more. Season again.

6 Re-roll the pastry disc until slightly larger than the top of your dish. Brush beaten egg on to the exposed edges of the pastry already in the dish and place the pastry lid on top. Press the edges to seal. Cut a little hole, 1cm in diameter, in the top. If you want, you can make little imprints around the edge to add some interest, then brush once more with egg and place the pie in the oven on the hot baking sheet.

7 Bake the pie in the oven for 20 minutes, then reduce the temperature to 180°C/fan 160°C/gas mark 4 and bake for a further 1 hour 20 minutes. Allow the pie to sit for 20 minutes or so before serving with a crunchy green salad.

TIP

If you are a fish lover you can lay smoked or peppered mackerel fillets in between the layers of potato and onion and continue with the recipe.

hot-smoked
salmon **GOUGÈRE**

Gougère is a baked cheesy choux pastry. It is straightforward to make but looks incredible when it arrives at the table. I can imagine nothing better than eating this for a celebration Sunday brunch with a glass of bubbly – on Mother's Day perhaps (hint, hint).

**SERVES
4**

EQUIPMENT
**1 x shallow round or oval ovenproof pie dish,
1.5-litre capacity**

FOR THE FILLING AND TOPPING
45g butter, plus a little extra for greasing
30g plain flour
400ml whole milk
70g mature Cheddar cheese, grated
1 small bunch of fresh flat-leaf parsley,
   leaves chopped
Grated zest of 1 lemon
300g hot-smoked salmon, skin removed,
   thickly flaked
10g dried breadcrumbs

FOR THE CHEESY GOUGÈRE
70g plain flour
¼ tsp salt
A pinch of cayenne pepper
60g unsalted butter, chilled and diced
2 medium eggs, lightly whisked
45g mature Cheddar cheese, grated

1 First make the filling: melt the butter in a pan over a low-medium heat. When it's foaming, add the flour and mix with a wooden spoon until smooth. Cook for 1 minute. Gradually add the milk, stirring to make a smooth sauce, then bring to a simmer and cook for 1 minute. Remove the sauce from the heat, add the cheese, parsley, lemon zest and salmon, and set aside.

2 To make the cheesy gougère, sift the flour with the salt and cayenne pepper on to a sheet of non-stick baking paper. Melt the butter in a pan with 150ml water, bring to the boil, then pour in the flour using the baking paper as a funnel. Remove from the heat and beat really vigorously with a wooden spoon for a minute or until the mixture is smooth and comes away from the sides of the pan. Set aside to cool.

3 Preheat the oven to 220°C/fan 200°C/gas mark 7.

4 Gradually beat the eggs into the cooled gougère mixture, so that it becomes smooth and shiny and drops off the spoon rather reluctantly, then stir in the cheese. Grease the pie dish, then spoon in the gougère mixture around the edges, pushing it up against the sides of the dish. Don't panic if it all looks a bit messy and sticky. Leave a well in the centre of the dish.

5 Spoon your fishy filling into the well in the middle of the dish, sprinkle over the breadcrumbs and bake for 35 minutes or until the gougère is puffed up and golden.

roasted risotto pumpkin <u>PIE</u>

EQUIPMENT
1 x 1.5-litre ovenproof dish

1 small pumpkin or queen squash (about 1kg)
1 tbsp olive oil, plus a little extra for frying the
    sage leaves
15g unsalted butter
1–2 shallots, depending on their size, finely chopped
1 garlic clove, crushed
100g butternut squash, peeled, deseeded and
    chopped into bite-sized cubes
150g Arborio risotto rice
A small bunch of fresh sage, half roughly chopped,
    remaining leaves reserved for garnish
200ml white wine
400ml vegetable stock (gluten free, if necessary)
30g Parmesan cheese, finely grated (or
    vegetarian alternative)
Salt and freshly ground black pepper

The clever thing about this pie is that there's no need to make pastry, as the pumpkin acts as a delicious container for the risotto, which is baked in the oven rather than the usual endless stirring on the hob. The pumpkin makes a great centrepiece for a vegetarian Christmas dinner. Oh, and it's gluten free too.

1 Preheat the oven to 200°C/fan 180°C/gas mark 6. Start by slicing off the top of the pumpkin to make a lid or hat and place in a large, shallow roasting tin. Scoop out the seeds from the pumpkin and hollow out some of the flesh to create the container for the risotto. Rub the pumpkin with a tablespoon of the olive oil and season with salt and pepper. Place in the roasting tin along with the lid and bake for 35 minutes. Remove from the oven and set aside.

2 Turn the oven down to 170°C/ fan 150°C/gas mark 3½. Put the ovenproof dish into the oven to warm.

3 Melt the butter in a medium non-stick frying pan over a medium heat, add the shallots and fry for 5–7 minutes or until softened and golden. Add the garlic and butternut squash and stir well, then add the rice and the chopped sage (remember to save the whole leaves for later). Make sure all the ingredients are evenly coated in the butter.

4 Add the wine and stock and bring up to a gentle simmer. As soon as you have reached this point, tip the risotto into the warm ovenproof dish and bake uncovered for 30 minutes. Remove from the oven and stir in the Parmesan (or vegetarian alternative). Spoon the risotto into the roasted pumpkin and bake for 15–20 minutes or until the pumpkin container is warm.

5 While the filled pumpkin is warming through, heat a glug of olive oil in a nonstick pan and fry the sage leaves over a high heat.

6 Just before serving, top the risotto with the sage leaves. Manoeuvre the pumpkin onto a plate or board and finish by placing the lid on top at a jaunty angle.

rösti-topped chicken and pancetta **PIE**

SERVES
6–8

EQUIPMENT
1 large ovenproof pie dish, approx. 2.5 litres

1 x 1.8–2kg whole chicken
1 carrot, 2 celery sticks, ½ an onion, a few
   peppercorns, for making the stock
1.25kg floury potatoes (about 5 large ones)
225g cubed pancetta
250g chestnut mushrooms, cut into quarters
125g butter, plus extra for frying
800g leeks, cut into fat rounds, 1–2cm thick
3 tbsp roughly chopped fresh tarragon leaves
3 tbsp plain flour
250ml double cream
Salt and freshly ground black pepper

This pie is well worth the effort. You will need to cook
a chicken and make some stock, but don't be put off. It's
brilliant for feeding a crowd, and appeals to children as well
as grown-ups. It also freezes well. If you are in a hurry you
can buy a roast chicken instead of cooking your own and use
600ml good-quality bought chicken stock.

1 Place the chicken and the stock ingredients into a large saucepan.
Cover with cold water and bring to the boil. Cover with a lid and simmer
for about 1 hour 20 minutes or until the chicken legs are wobbly and the
juices run clear when the flesh is pierced with a skewer. Carefully lift the
chicken out of the pan and set aside to cool.

2 Now reduce the stock by simmering the liquid with the lid off for about
1 hour (depending on the size of your pan and how much water you put
in at the beginning). Continue until about 600ml of liquid remains.

3 Preheat the oven to 200°C/fan 180°C/gas mark 6. Wash the potatoes,
place on a baking sheet and bake in the oven for about 45 minutes or
until just beginning to soften but not cooked through. Leave until cool
enough to handle, then peel away the skins and coarsely grate the flesh
into a bowl. Season with salt and pepper. Leave the oven on.

4 Meanwhile, fry the pancetta in a large frying pan over a high heat until
just crisp, then remove and set aside. Fry the mushrooms in the fat left
in the pan for a couple of minutes, adding a little butter if necessary.
Set aside.

continued...

TIP
You can prepare this ahead, prior to baking. Then either keep
in the fridge for up to 24 hours or freeze immediately once
assembled then thaw overnight before cooking. If it has been
frozen, you may need to increase the cooking time to 1 hour.

rösti-topped chicken
and pancetta **PIE**
continued...

5 In a separate pan, melt 50g of the butter and add the leeks and tarragon. Cover with a lid and leave to soften on a low heat for about 10 minutes. Stir in the flour and cook, stirring, for 2–3 minutes, then add your 600ml stock. Bring to the boil, stirring all the time, then reduce the heat and simmer for about 2 minutes or until the sauce has just thickened slightly. Remove from the heat and stir in the cream. Leave the sauce to cool.

6 Remove the flesh from the chicken and roughly chop, discarding the skin. Stir into the cooled sauce with the pancetta and mushrooms. Taste and season with salt and black pepper as necessary. Spoon into your ovenproof dish.

7 Place mounds of grated potato on top of the chicken mixture, then melt the remaining butter and pour over the top. Stand the dish on a baking sheet and bake in the oven for 40 minutes or until golden and piping hot.

bonfire pumpkin
<u>PIE</u> with harissa

SERVES
8

EQUIPMENT
1 large deep-sided roasting tin,
approx. 35cm x 26cm

1 quantity of Spiced Tomato Sauce (see page 203)
1 small pumpkin or 1 medium butternut squash,
    peeled and deseeded
3 large parsnips, scrubbed and trimmed
2 red peppers, deseeded
1 red onion, cut into wedges
2–3 tbsp harissa paste (we like the Belazu brand)
2 tbsp olive oil
1 small bunch of fresh coriander, leaves chopped
50g unsalted butter
½ tsp smoked paprika, plus extra for sprinkling
6 sheets of filo pastry
Salt and freshly ground black pepper

FOR THE YOGHURT DIP
250ml full-fat natural yoghurt
1 large garlic clove, crushed
A small bunch of fresh mint, leaves roughly chopped
A squeeze of lemon juice

My father-in-law claims he would prefer barbecues if they were held indoors, with no smoke getting in your eyes and no summer bugs nipping at your ankles! I feel rather the same way about bonfire parties and drizzle. So at Higgidy we toast the arrival of autumn with this delicious, warming pie that can be eaten at home in front of the fire – no raincoat required.

1 Preheat the oven to 200°C/fan 180°C/gas mark 6. Make the Spiced Tomato Sauce according to the method on page 203.

2 Meanwhile, cut the pumpkin (or squash), parsnips and peppers into 3cm chunks and put into a large bowl with the onion wedges. Add the harissa paste, olive oil and 1 teaspoon of salt and mix well. Spread evenly over your roasting tin and pop into the oven for 30 minutes.

3 Remove the roasted vegetables from the oven and stir in the spiced tomato sauce, along with the chopped coriander and 100ml water.

4 Melt the butter with the paprika in a small pan over a medium heat. Brush a sheet of filo with the paprika butter and lay it over the roasted vegetables. Brush the remaining sheets of filo with the butter, loosely scrunch them up and place them on top of the first piece of filo. Brush any remaining butter over the top and sprinkle with extra paprika.

5 Bake in the oven for 25–30 minutes or until the filo is golden and crisp and the filling is piping hot.

6 Meanwhile, mix the yoghurt in a bowl with the garlic, mint and lemon juice. Season with salt and pepper and serve alongside the pie.

TIP
This goes down well at a bonfire party with a bowl of warm couscous and a pile of sticky sausages.

crafty
QUICHES
& trusty
TARTS

courgetti and ricotta **CHEESECAKES** with pink peppercorns

MAKES
10

EQUIPMENT
10 x 10cm round fluted tartlet tins;
1 x 12cm round pastry cutter

1 quantity of Quick Soured Cream Pastry
 (see page 217)
A little plain flour, for dusting
200g feta cheese
200g ricotta cheese
100g crème fraîche
2 medium eggs
2 medium egg yolks
50g frozen petits pois
2 spring onions, finely chopped
2 tbsp finely chopped fresh chives
2 tbsp finely chopped fresh mint
2 tbsp lemon juice
1 courgette, spiralised or grated
Whole pink peppercorns, for sprinkling
Salt and freshly ground black pepper

With a filling of ricotta, peas and garden herbs, these are a lighter take on a baked cheesecake and have summer written all over them. If there is a better use for courgetti, I am yet to find it. This recipe uses my Quick Soured Cream Pastry (see page 217), so it's super simple to make.

1 Make the quick soured cream pastry according to the method on page 217 and put in the fridge to rest for 30 minutes before using.

2 Preheat the oven to 200°C/fan 180°C/gas mark 6 and place a baking sheet in the oven to preheat. On a lightly floured work surface, roll out the pastry to about 3mm thick. Cut or stamp out ten 12cm circles using the pastry cutter, press each into a tartlet tin and trim the excess from the edges with a sharp knife.

3 Now make the filling. Weigh 150g of the feta into a large bowl and break it up with a fork, then stir in the ricotta and crème fraîche. Beat well until evenly combined, or you could do this in a food processor to save time. Add the whole eggs and egg yolks and mix well, then add the petits pois, spring onions, fresh herbs and lemon juice and mix well again. Season with salt and pepper.

4 Divide the filling mixture between the lined tartlet tins and top with the courgette, the remaining feta and a sprinkle of pink peppercorns.

5 Transfer the tartlet tins onto the hot baking sheet and place on the middle shelf of the oven. Lower the heat to 160°C/fan 140°C/gas mark 3 and bake for 35 minutes or until set and the feta is just golden. Allow to cool slightly before removing the cheesecakes from the tins – you may need to use a knife to loosen the edges. Serve warm or cold.

wintry **QUICHE**
with walnutty pastry

**SERVES
6**

One of our staple family suppers is sausages, heaps of steaming kale cabbage and buttery mash. We thought we'd try the sausage and kale combo in a quiche – it really works!

EQUIPMENT
1 loose-bottomed fluted rectangular tart tin,
30cm x 20cm

FOR THE WALNUT PASTRY
40g walnuts
200g plain flour, plus a little for dusting
½ tsp salt
100g unsalted butter, chilled and diced
1 medium egg, beaten

FOR THE FILLING
90g kale, shredded
2 tbsp olive oil
1 large leek, sliced
1 red onion, finely sliced
2 garlic cloves, finely chopped
½ tsp dried chilli flakes
8 chipolata sausages
500ml double cream
2 medium eggs and 2 egg yolks, whisked
1 tbsp Dijon mustard
55g mature Cheddar cheese, finely grated
Salt and freshly ground black pepper

1 For the pastry, whizz the walnuts in a food processor with 2 tablespoons of the flour until finely ground, then add the remaining flour and the salt and whizz again to mix. Now add the butter and pulse until it looks like fine breadcrumbs. Add the egg and pulse quickly until the pastry just starts to come together. Tip on to a lightly floured work surface and shape into a disc. Wrap in clingfilm and chill for 30 minutes.

2 On a lightly floured work surface, roll out the pastry to about 3mm thick and big enough to line your tin. Press the pastry carefully into the tin, making sure the edges sit just proud of the rim, and trim the excess pastry. Prick the base all over with a fork and chill for 30 minutes.

3 Preheat the oven to 200°C/fan 180°C/gas mark 6 and put a baking sheet in to heat up.

4 Remove the tart tin from the fridge, line with crumpled non-stick baking paper and fill with baking beans (see page 211). Place on the hot baking sheet in the oven and cook for 20 minutes, then remove the paper and beans, and return to the oven for a further 10 minutes. Set aside, leaving the oven switched on.

continued...

wintry **QUICHE**
with walnutty pastry
continued...

5 Bring a pan of salted water to the boil and blanch the kale for 2–3 minutes or until tender. Drain, then run it under cold water, drain again well and set aside.

6 Heat half the oil in a large pan over a low heat and add the leek and onion. Season with salt and pepper and cook for 10 minutes to soften. Stir in the garlic and chilli flakes and continue to cook for a couple of minutes more. Then spoon into a bowl and set aside to cool.

7 Add the remaining oil to the empty pan, set over a medium heat and cook the chipolatas until browned all over and cooked through. Remove and set aside to cool.

8 Whisk together the cream, eggs and egg yolks, mustard, two-thirds of the cheese and some salt and pepper. Spoon the onion, leek and kale over the base of your tart case. Top with the chipolatas and pour over the cream mix. Sprinkle over the remaining cheese. Carefully transfer to the hot baking sheet in the oven and cook for 40 minutes or until golden and set. Remove and leave to stand for 5 minutes before serving.

baby new potato, leek and goat's cheese **TART**

SERVES 6

EQUIPMENT

1 x 23cm loose-bottomed round tart tin

1 quantity of Savoury Shortcrust Pastry
  (see page 212 or use ready-made pastry)
A little plain flour, for dusting

FOR THE FILLING

50g butter
325g leeks, stripped of tough outer leaves, halved
  lengthways and sliced into 5mm crescents
2 tsp roughly chopped fresh sage
1 tbsp Dijon mustard
2 tbsp cider vinegar
3 medium eggs
225ml double cream
250g baby new potatoes, each cut in half, parboiled
125g soft goat's cheese
Salt and freshly ground black pepper

This lovely, chunky 'all-in-one' tart will satisfy even the heartiest appetite. Be bold and serve with nothing but a few salad leaves and a glass of chilled cider.

1 Make the savoury shortcrust pastry according to the method on page 212 and put in the fridge to rest for 30 minutes before using.

2 On a lightly floured surface, roll out the pastry to about 3mm thick and line your tin with it, making sure the edge of the pastry stands a little proud above the rim. Trim the edges, prick the base with a fork and return to the fridge for 30 minutes. Don't be tempted to skip this step – it helps stop the pastry shrinking in the oven.

3 Preheat the oven to 200°C/fan 180°C/gas mark 6 and put a baking sheet in to heat up. Melt the butter in a large shallow pan over a low heat and add the leeks and sage. Cover and cook for about 15 minutes until soft but not coloured. Stir in the mustard, vinegar and a pinch of salt and pepper, and continue to cook for a minute or two until the liquid has evaporated.

4 Remove the tart tin from the fridge, line it with crumpled non-stick baking paper, and fill with baking beans (see page 211). Bake on the hot baking sheet for 20 minutes, then remove the paper and beans and return to the oven for a further 5 minutes. Remove and reduce the oven to 190°C/fan 170°C/gas mark 5.

5 Crack the eggs into a large bowl and gently beat in the cream until smooth. Add the mustardy leeks and parboiled potatoes and tip the whole lot into the pastry case. Top with lumps of goat's cheese and season with pepper.

6 Place back on the hot baking sheet and bake for 25 minutes, then increase the oven temperature to 200°C/fan 180°C/gas mark 6 and bake for another 10 minutes or until the tart is a lovely golden brown. Serve hot, warm or cold.

three-onion
PISSALADIÉRE

SERVES
6

This is a gutsy French classic to which we've added some sun-dried tomatoes. If you don't like anchovies, you can substitute with slices of ripe goat's cheese and plenty of extra black pepper.

EQUIPMENT

1 shallow rectangular baking tray, approx. 33cm x 22cm

2 tbsp olive oil

A generous knob of butter

2 red onions, sliced

2 large white onions, sliced

6 small shallots, cut into wedges

2 large garlic cloves, finely chopped

1 small bunch of fresh thyme, leaves stripped

A little plain flour, for dusting

375g all-butter puff pastry

2 large sun-dried tomatoes in olive oil, drained and thinly sliced

Approx. 15 pitted black olives, halved

1 x 50g tin of anchovy fillets in olive oil, drained and cut in half lengthways

1 medium egg, lightly beaten

Salt and freshly ground black pepper

1 Heat the oil and butter in a large frying pan over a low heat. Add the red and white onions and the shallots along with a good pinch of salt and pepper. Cover with a lid and cook for 20 minutes or until soft.

2 Uncover the pan, increase the heat and continue to cook for a further 10 minutes, stirring, until golden. Stir in the garlic and most of the thyme and cook for a final minute, then spoon into a bowl and set aside to cool completely.

3 Preheat the oven to 200°C/fan 180°C/gas mark 6 and put a baking sheet in to heat up. (Your cold baking tray with the pissaladière will need to sit on this to help conduct the heat and cook the pastry.)

4 On a lightly floured work surface, roll out your pastry to about 2mm thick and trim it to fit your baking tray. Score a border around the edge, about 2cm in from the sides. Spoon the golden onions over the centre of your pastry, spreading them out to the border in an even layer. Scatter with the sun-dried tomatoes and olives, then lay the anchovy fillets over the top in a lattice pattern.

5 Brush the pastry border with a little beaten egg and place the baking tray in the oven, on the hot baking sheet. Bake for 25–30 minutes or until the pastry is golden and crisp. Sprinkle with a few more fresh thyme leaves and serve.

three ways
with <u>TARTINES</u>

MAKES 3 TARTINES

The thing that keeps me going back to this recipe, time and again, is that I can tailor it to almost any occasion – simply by changing the toppings. I've suggested three of my favourite combinations, but feel free to improvise and express yourself. Oh, and if you'd like to learn my sneaky secret to a seriously crisp puff pastry base, read on.

FOR THE BASE

A little plain flour, for dusting

500g all-butter puff pastry (check the label
   if making a vegan option)

A little vegetable oil, for greasing

1 On a lightly floured work surface, roll out the puff pastry into a rectangle measuring 45cm x 25cm, about 3mm thick. Cut the pastry into three smaller rectangles. Prick the pastry rectangles with a fork, place on a lightly oiled baking sheet and put into the fridge to chill for 20 minutes.

2 Preheat the oven to 220°C/fan 200°C/gas mark 7. Remove the pastry from the fridge and place a second lightly oiled baking sheet directly on top, oiled side touching the pastry (this weighs down the pastry to make it crisp). Bake for 15 minutes, then remove from the oven, take off the top baking sheet and set aside to cool. Finish with your choice of topping. Here are three of our favourites...

FOR A LAZY BUT LOVELY SUNDAY BRUNCH
Wrap avocado wedges in thinly sliced smoked bacon and bake in a hot oven for about 15 minutes until the bacon is crisp. Stir a generous spoonful of sun-dried tomato paste into some ricotta cheese. Spread over the baked tartines and top with the crispy bacon and avocado wedges.

A WONDERFUL 'WINGING-IT' WEDNESDAY SUPPER
Using a potato peeler, cut a courgette into ribbon-like strips. Place in a bowl with the grated zest and juice of 1 lemon, a crushed garlic clove, salt, freshly ground black pepper and a good slug of olive oil. Thickly spread the baked tartines with a creamy goat's cheese, pile the dressed courgette on top and scatter with pea shoots.

THE 'WHAT-TO-SERVE-MY-VEGAN-FRIEND' LUNCH
Bake a couple of scrubbed medium-sized sweet potatoes until tender. Cut in half lengthways, scoop the flesh into a bowl and mash with a small handful of chopped coriander, a chopped spring onion and a squeeze of lime juice. Spread over the baked tartines and top with a diced red chilli. Scatter with coriander leaves, drizzle with a little chilli oil and serve with a dollop of soured cream, or without for vegan guests.

cheddar ploughman
TARTLETS

MAKES
6

EQUIPMENT
6 x 10cm fluted round tartlet tins

1 quantity of Savoury Shortcrust Pastry
   (see page 212 or use ready-made pastry)
A little plain flour, for dusting
1 tbsp olive oil
1 onion, finely chopped
1 medium egg and 1 egg yolk, whisked
200ml double cream
100g mature Cheddar cheese, finely grated
50g dried breadcrumbs (blitz a piece of toast to
   fine crumbs in the food processor)
2 tsp sun-dried tomato paste
6 tbsp tomato chutney
6 cherry tomatoes, with green tufts left on
Salt and freshly ground black pepper

Inspired by the classic ploughman's combo of strong salty
Cheddar and sweet chutney, these make good picnic fodder
(either cold or still a little warm), or a great simple lunch
with a crisp green salad.

1 Make the savoury shortcrust pastry according to the method on page
212 and put in the fridge to rest for 30 minutes before using.

2 On a lightly floured work surface, roll out the pastry to about 2mm
thick. Cut out six 15cm circles and line your tartlet tins with them. Prick
the bases with a fork, then chill for 30 minutes.

3 Preheat the oven to 200°C/fan 180°C/gas mark 6 and put in a baking
sheet to heat up. Heat the oil in a frying pan over a medium heat, add
the onion and cook for 8 minutes to soften, then remove and set aside
to cool.

4 Whisk the whole egg and egg yolk with the cream and two-thirds
of the Cheddar cheese, then season well with salt and pepper and
set aside. Mix the breadcrumbs with the tomato paste and remaining
cheese and set aside.

5 Place a spoonful of chutney in the middle of each tart case, spoon
the onions over the top, then pour over the egg filling. Thickly sprinkle
with the breadcrumbs and Cheddar mixture and finally top with a whole
cherry tomato, pressing it slightly into the filling.

6 Reduce the oven to 190°C/fan 170°C/gas mark 5 and place the tartlets
in the oven on the hot baking sheet. Bake for 35–40 minutes until the
filling has set and the top is crispy and golden. Cool slightly, then turn
out of the tins and serve with a crisp salad.

roasted sweet potato, chorizo and chard QUICHE

EQUIPMENT

1 x 23cm loose-bottomed deep round tart tin

FOR THE SWEET POTATO BASE

500g sweet potato, peeled and cut into chunks

½ tsp dried chilli flakes

¼ tsp ground coriander

¼ tsp ground cumin

2 tbsp olive oil

220g rice flour, plus extra for dusting

2 tsp xanthan gum

1 medium egg, beaten

Salt and freshly ground black pepper

FOR THE FILLING

2 tbsp olive oil

1 red pepper, deseeded and thickly sliced

1 orange pepper, deseeded and thickly sliced

1 red onion, finely chopped

1 large garlic clove, finely chopped

100g chorizo sausage, diced (check the label
if making for gluten-free guests)

100g chard or spinach leaves, roughly chopped

2 medium eggs

2 medium egg yolks

200ml unsweetened soya cream (or soya milk
if you can't find cream)

125g soft creamy goat's cheese (optional)

Here's a recipe to wow your gluten-free friends. The pastry is made from roasted sweet potato and rice flour and I've combined the remaining sweet potato with chard, chilli and smoky chorizo for a deeply satisfying quiche.

1 Preheat oven to 200°C/fan 180°C/gas mark 6. Cut a circle of non-stick baking paper about 28cm in diameter and use to line the base and sides of the tart tin.

2 Toss the sweet potato with the chilli flakes, ground spices and the olive oil in a bowl. Season generously with salt and pepper. Scatter evenly over a baking tray and roast in the oven for 25 minutes or until soft. Remove from the oven and leave to cool. Meanwhile, turn the oven down to 190°C/fan 170°C/gas mark 5.

3 When the potato is cool, mash 300g of it (reserve the rest for the filling) with a potato masher in a bowl, or use a food processor for a finer texture. Add the rice flour, xanthan gum and beaten egg and mix to form a dough, or add them to the food processor and pulse until the ingredients come together. The dough should be soft but not sticky, so add a tablespoon of water if it's too dry or a little flour if it's too sticky. Wrap the dough in clingfilm and place in the fridge to rest for a minimum of 30 minutes. (The dough can be stored in the fridge for up to 24 hours, but you may need to roll it in some flour if it has become sticky.)

4 For the filling, toss the peppers in a tablespoon of the olive oil in a baking tray and roast for 20 minutes, or until they have just caught around the edges. Meanwhile, heat another tablespoon of olive oil in a frying pan over a medium heat. Add the red onion and garlic and fry for a few minutes or until the onion is softened and has a golden tinge. Add half the chorizo (reserve the rest to scatter over the top of the quiche) and fry for 1 minute. Add the chard (or spinach), cover and cook over a low heat for 1–2 minutes or until just wilted. Leave to cool.

continued...

roasted sweet potato, chorizo and chard QUICHE
continued...

5 Put a baking sheet in the oven to heat up. Remove the dough from the fridge and roll into a circle, about 3mm thick, on a lightly floured surface (use rice flour). Carefully place on the base of the tart tin and line, making sure the edges of the pasty stand just a little proud above the rim, then trim away any excess.

6 Crack the whole eggs into a bowl, add the egg yolks and soya cream and season with salt and pepper. Give the ingredients a really good stir to make sure they are evenly mixed together.

7 Scatter the chorizo and chard mixture over the dough base, top with the reserved roasted sweet potato and peppers and pour over the egg mixture. Top with the reserved chorizo and the goat's cheese in pieces (if using). Place on the hot baking sheet and bake for 25–30 minutes or until the filling is set. Leave to cool slightly before removing from the tin to serve.

EQUIPMENT
8 x 10cm round tartlet tins

1 quantity of Quick Soured Cream Pastry
  (see page 217)
A little plain flour, for dusting
12 medium tomatoes
2 tbsp fresh herbs (such as thyme and oregano),
  very roughly chopped
1 tsp dried chilli flakes
3 tbsp olive oil, plus more for drizzling
A generous knob of butter
400g shallots, thinly sliced
80g feta cheese, crumbled
Salt and freshly ground black pepper
Sprigs of fresh thyme, to garnish

slow-roast tomato **TARTLETS**
with soured cream pastry

When I was a child, my mum grew tomatoes in a greenhouse at the end of our garden. The tomato plants were cared for, watered daily and even talked to. I became almost jealous of them, until the middle of summer when I was allowed to pick an abundance. I remember the smell – all gardeny – and how sweet they tasted. I've created these tartlets in their honour.

1 Make the quick soured cream pastry according to the method on page 217 and put it into the fridge to rest for 30 minutes before using.

2 On a lightly floured work surface, roll out the pastry to about 3mm thick. Cut or stamp out eight 15cm circles and line your tartlet tins with them. Prick the bases with a fork and chill for 30 minutes.

3 Preheat the oven to 160°C/fan 140°C/gas mark 3. Halve the tomatoes and place in a bowl with the herbs, chilli flakes and olive oil. Season with salt and black pepper and toss until the tomatoes are well coated. Spread the tomatoes evenly on a large baking sheet and bake in the oven for about 40 minutes or until beginning to slightly shrivel. Remove and set aside. Increase the oven to 200°C/fan 180°C/gas mark 6 and put in a baking sheet to heat up.

4 Melt a generous knob of butter in a large pan over a low heat. Add the shallots, put a lid on the pan and cook for about 15 minutes or until very soft. Remove the lid, increase the heat and cook for about 5 minutes more or until beginning to caramelise. Set aside to cool.

5 Divide the cooled buttery shallots between the pastry cases and spread out with the back of a spoon, allowing a 1cm border at the edge. Sprinkle over the feta, then arrange three tomato halves over the top and season again with salt and black pepper.

6 Drizzle with a little olive oil, and bake on the hot baking sheet in the centre of the oven for 30 minutes or until golden. Allow to cool slightly, then carefully remove from the tartlet tins. Top with sprigs of fresh thyme.

salmon and watercress **QUICHE** with pink peppercorns

**SERVES
6**

EQUIPMENT

**1 loose-bottomed fluted rectangular tart tin,
30cm x 20cm**

1 quantity of Savoury Shortcrust Pastry
   (see page 212 or use ready-made pastry)
A little plain flour, for dusting

FOR THE FILLING

3 salmon fillets (approx. 350g)
Juice of ½ a lemon
A good knob of unsalted butter
1 medium onion, finely sliced
200g new potatoes, ideally Jersey Royals,
   cut into 1.5cm chunks and parboiled
50g watercress (leaves picked and any tough
   stalks discarded), finely chopped
2 tbsp chopped fresh dill leaves
3 medium eggs, whisked
300ml double cream
½ tsp pink peppercorns, lightly crushed
Salt and freshly ground black pepper

This quiche is a nod to spring, when delicious watercress comes into season. Pastel colours make an appearance in the hedgerows and in our wardrobes, and everything looks pretty. This is a fabulous recipe to serve up on an Easter table or at a sunny spring picnic.

1 Make the savoury shortcrust pastry according to the method on page 212 and put in the fridge to rest for 30 minutes before using.

2 On a lightly floured work surface, roll out the pastry to about 3mm thick and line your tart tin with it, making sure the edge of the pastry stands just a little proud above the rim. Trim the edges, then prick the base with a fork and return it to the fridge for a further 30 minutes. Don't be tempted to skip this step – it helps stop the pastry shrinking in the oven.

3 Preheat the oven to 200°C/180°C/gas mark 6 and put a baking sheet in to heat up. Tear off a sheet of foil big enough to enclose all your salmon fillets and lay it on a work surface. Put the salmon in the middle, add the lemon juice and some salt and pepper, and scrunch to seal tightly. Bake in the oven for 12 minutes, then remove and set aside to cool.

continued...

salmon and watercress **QUICHE** with pink peppercorns
continued...

4 Take the pastry case out of the fridge, line with crumpled non-stick baking paper and fill with baking beans (see page 211). Place in the oven on the hot baking sheet and bake for 20 minutes. Then remove the paper and beans and return the case to the oven for a further 5 minutes. This will allow the pastry base to dry out before you pile in the filling.

5 Reduce the oven to 180°C/160°C fan/gas mark 4. Melt the butter in a frying pan over a medium heat. Add the onion and let it soften for 8 minutes. Remove from the heat and leave to cool, then spoon into the pastry case. Thickly flake the salmon (discarding the skin) and scatter it over the onions with the parboiled potatoes and most of the chopped watercress and dill.

6 Whisk together the eggs and cream, season well with salt and pour into the pastry case. Scatter with the remaining watercress and dill and the peppercorns. Place on the hot baking sheet in the oven and bake for 30 minutes or until the filling has just set and the top is turning golden.

smoked bacon
TARTIFLETTES

**SERVES
6**

EQUIPMENT
6 x 10cm deep round tartlet tins

1 quantity of Savoury Shortcrust Pastry
   (see page 212 or use ready-made pastry)
500g small unpeeled waxy potatoes, such
   as Charlotte
A little plain flour, for dusting
1 tbsp olive oil
6 rashers of streaky smoked bacon, cut into lardons
1 large onion, finely chopped
1 large garlic clove, finely chopped
50g mature Cheddar cheese, finely grated
50g Gruyère cheese, finely grated
200g crème fraîche
100g double cream
40g dried breadcrumbs (blitz a piece of toast to fine
   crumbs in a food processor)
Salt and freshly ground black pepper

**Tartiflette is a French dish often served in the mountains.
It is simple but rich, and the secret to making it work well
is baked potatoes. Traditionally it's served with cold meats
and gherkins, but we like to pair it with a simple salad of
peppery leaves.**

1 Make the savoury shortcrust pastry according to the method on page
212 and put in the fridge to rest for 30 minutes before using.

2 Preheat the oven to 200°C/fan 180°C/gas mark 6 and put a baking
sheet in to heat up. Give the potatoes a wash, pop them on a baking
tray and bake for 35–45 minutes, depending on size. Remove from the
oven (leaving it switched on) and, when cool enough to handle, peel
away the skins. Break the potatoes into rough pieces, place in a large
bowl and set aside.

3 Meanwhile, on a lightly floured work surface, roll out the pastry to
about 2mm thick. Cut out six 15cm circles and line your tartlet tins with
them. Prick the bases with a fork and chill for 30 minutes.

4 Heat the oil in a frying pan over a medium-high heat and add the bacon.
Cook for 5 minutes, then add the onion and fry for another 5 minutes
or until just golden. Add the garlic and fry for a further minute. Add the
contents of the frying pan to the potatoes, along with two-thirds of the
cheeses, the crème fraîche and cream. Season generously with salt and
pepper and mix well.

5 Heap the potato mixture into your tartlet cases. Mix the breadcrumbs
with the rest of the cheeses and sprinkle over. Put the tartlets into the
oven on the hot baking sheet, immediately lower the temperature to
190°C/fan 170°C/gas mark 5 and bake for 35–40 minutes (covering with
foil if they start to brown too much) or until the filling is piping hot and the
pastry is cooked through.

roasted beetroot
GALETTE

SERVES
6

This is a beautiful tart made with a little hot horseradish spread on buttery puff pastry and topped with a layer of multi-coloured beets. Beetroot has many health benefits, but one of its earliest uses was as an aphrodisiac during Roman times. Perhaps this could be made as a starter for a Valentine's supper?

1 uncooked French golden beetroot, scrubbed clean
1 uncooked French candy beetroot, scrubbed clean
2 cooked purple beetroots
30g butter
A little plain flour, for dusting
250g all-butter puff pastry
125g mascarpone
25g hot horseradish cream
A little olive oil, for brushing
A few fresh thyme leaves
1 tbsp runny honey, warmed
Salt and freshly ground black pepper

1 Start by preparing your beetroots; slice each one as thinly as you are able, 2–3mm thick. Over a low heat, melt the butter in a large frying pan and add the uncooked golden and candy beetroot slices.

2 Cut out a circle of non-stick baking paper, roughly the size of your frying pan. Scrunch it up and spread it out again into a crinkled paper circle (this helps trap steam to aid the cooking process). Lay it over your beetroot slices and allow to steam for 8 minutes or until just soft. Set aside to cool slightly.

3 Preheat the oven to 200°C/fan 180°C/gas mark 6. On a lightly floured work surface, roll out the pastry to a rectangle measuring roughly 20cm x 30cm, about 3mm thick. Transfer it to a baking sheet and score a 2cm border around the edge using a sharp knife, making sure not to cut through the pastry.

4 Place the mascarpone in a small bowl and mix to soften, then stir in the horseradish until evenly distributed. Season with a little salt and pepper. Spread the mascarpone mixture over the puff pastry, taking care not to go beyond the scored border. Top with a mixture of the softened beetroot and the ready-cooked beetroot slices. Brush each slice with olive oil, sprinkle over the thyme leaves, and bake for 30 minutes.

5 Remove from the oven and allow to cool slightly, then brush with warm honey just before serving.

our best **QUICHE** lorraine

**SERVES
6**

EQUIPMENT
1 x 23cm loose-bottomed fluted round tart tin

1 quantity of Savoury Shortcrust Pastry
  (see page 212 or use ready-made pastry)
A little plain flour, for dusting

FOR THE FILLING
1 tbsp olive oil
125g smoked bacon lardons
1 medium onion, roughly chopped
3 garlic cloves, finely chopped
3 medium eggs
250ml double cream
125g Gruyère cheese, grated
50g thinly sliced pancetta
Salt and cracked black pepper

The world's most popular quiche. Enough said!

1 Make the savoury shortcrust pastry according to the method on page 212 and put in the fridge to rest for 30 minutes before using.

2 On a lightly floured work surface, roll out the pastry to about 3mm thick and line your tart tin with it, making sure the edge of the pastry stands just a little proud above the rim. Trim the edges, then prick the base with a fork and return it to the fridge for a further 30 minutes. Don't be tempted to skip this step – it will help stop the pastry shrinking in the oven.

3 Meanwhile, heat the olive oil in a frying pan over a medium heat. When hot, add the bacon lardons and fry for 3 minutes or so. Add the onion and cook for another 3 minutes, then add the garlic and cook for a further 2 minutes or until the onion is soft and the bacon has begun to crisp up. Set aside to cool slightly.

4 Preheat the oven to 200°C/fan 180°C/gas mark 6 and put a baking sheet in to heat up. Remove the pastry case from the fridge, line with crumpled non-stick baking paper and fill with baking beans (see page 211). Bake in the oven on the hot baking sheet for 20 minutes, then remove the paper and beans and return to the oven for a further 5 minutes. This will allow the base to dry out before you pile in the filling.

continued...

TIP
To make a summery version of this quiche, add 50g sun-blushed tomatoes and 50g asparagus tips (cooked briefly in boiling water) at the same time as adding the pancetta in step 7. Bake as directed and garnish with fresh parsley.

our best **QUICHE** lorraine
continued...

5 Reduce the oven to 180°C/160°C fan/gas mark 4. Crack the eggs into a large bowl, add the cream and grated cheese and beat gently until you have a lovely creamy mixture. Season with cracked black pepper and carefully with salt – remember that the bacon and cheese are already quite salty.

6 Sprinkle the bacon and onion mixture into the base of the pastry case (along with any juices left in the pan), then gently pour over the eggy mixture. Carefully transfer to the hot baking sheet in the oven and bake for 20 minutes or until the mixture has only just begun to set.

7 Remove from the oven and, working quickly, top with the pancetta slices. Return the quiche to the oven and increase the temperature to 190°C/fan 170°C/gas mark 5. Bake for another 15 minutes or until the pancetta has just begun to turn crispy. Allow to cool for a few minutes before serving.

crispy club
TARTLETS

EQUIPMENT
6 x 10cm deep round fluted tartlet tins

1 quantity of Savoury Shortcrust Pastry
  (see page 212 or use ready-made pastry)
A little plain flour, for dusting

FOR THE FILLING
A splash of olive oil, for frying
1 x 100g pack of thinly sliced smoked pancetta
4 medium eggs, lightly whisked
130g full-fat crème fraîche
40g Gruyère cheese, finely grated
1½ tbsp Dijon mustard
1 medium chicken breast, cooked and sliced,
  skin removed
9 cherry tomatoes, halved
1 tbsp finely snipped fresh chives
Salt and freshly ground black pepper

Inspired by a well-loved sandwich, we've taken the best bits of the chicken and bacon club and crammed them into a simple shortcrust pastry case.

1 Make the savoury shortcrust pastry according to the method on page 212 and put in the fridge to rest for 30 minutes.

2 On a lightly floured work surface, roll out the pastry to about 2mm thick. Cut out six 15cm circles and line your tartlet tins with them. Prick the bases with a fork, then chill for 30 minutes.

3 Preheat the oven to 200°C/fan 180°C/gas mark 6 and put a baking sheet in to heat up. Remove the tartlet tins from the fridge, line with crumpled non-stick baking paper and fill with baking beans (see page 211). Bake in the oven on the hot baking sheet for 10–15 minutes, then remove the paper and beans and return to the oven for 5–8 minutes or until the pastry is dry and the edges are beginning to turn golden. Remove and reduce the oven to 190°C/fan 170°C/gas mark 5.

4 Heat the olive oil in a frying pan over a medium heat and sizzle the pancetta on both sides for just a moment. (No more, because it's going to be cooked again in the tartlets.) Set aside.

5 Whisk together the eggs, crème fraîche and Gruyère. Season with a little salt and black pepper.

6 Spread the mustard over the tartlet bases, then divide the chicken, crispy pancetta and cherry tomatoes between them, arranging them higgledy-piggledy – it's fine if the pancetta pokes up out of the tart cases a little. Pour over the crème fraîche mixture and scatter with the chives. Bake in the oven on the hot baking sheet for 15–20 minutes or until set.

lemony asparagus and ricotta **TART**

EQUIPMENT
1 x 23cm loose-bottomed fluted round tart tin

1 quantity of Savoury Shortcrust Pastry
  (see page 212 or use ready-made pastry)
A little plain flour, for dusting
1 egg yolk, beaten
Grated zest of 1 lemon, to serve

FOR THE FILLING
250g ricotta cheese
150g crème fraîche
50g Parmesan cheese, finely grated
1 small bunch of fresh dill, leaves chopped
Juice and grated zest of 1 lemon
200g asparagus spears, woody ends removed
75g podded fresh or frozen broad beans
Salt and freshly ground black pepper

FOR THE DRESSING
2 tbsp extra-virgin olive oil
A squeeze of lemon juice

This is a beautiful tart to celebrate the asparagus season. If you can't get hold of asparagus (its season is quite short), you can substitute with griddled courgette ribbons or roasted cherry tomatoes.

1 Make the savoury shortcrust pastry according to the method on page 212 and put in the fridge to rest for 30 minutes before using.

2 On a lightly floured surface, roll out the pastry to about 3mm thick and line your tart tin with it, making sure the edge of the pastry stands just a little proud above the rim. Trim the edges, then prick the base with a fork and return it to the fridge for a further 30 minutes. Don't skip this step – it will help prevent the pastry shrinking in the oven.

3 Preheat the oven to 200°C/fan 180°C/gas mark 6 and put a baking sheet in to heat up. Remove your tin from the fridge, line with crumpled non-stick baking paper and fill with baking beans (see page 211). Bake on the hot baking sheet in the oven for 20 minutes, then remove the paper and beans, brush with beaten egg yolk and bake for a further 10–15 minutes or until golden. Remove and let cool, then carefully remove the tin.

4 For the filling, beat together the ricotta and crème fraîche and stir in the Parmesan, dill, lemon zest and juice and a little salt and pepper. Bring a large pan of salted water to the boil. Cook the asparagus and broad beans for 2–3 minutes or until just tender, then drain and run under the cold tap to stop them cooking further. Squeeze the beans from their skins.

5 Once the tart case is completely cool, spoon in the creamy filling and arrange the asparagus and broad beans on top. Whisk the dressing ingredients together and brush or drizzle over the tart. Scatter with lemon zest and serve in thick slices.

cherry tomato
TARTE TATIN

This might look complicated, but in fact all you need are six main ingredients and a frying pan – so simple!

EQUIPMENT

1 x 23cm ovenproof non-stick frying pan or shallow fixed-base cake tin

A little plain flour, for dusting

375g all-butter puff pastry

600g cherry tomatoes (different colours, if available)

2–3 large garlic cloves, very finely chopped

2 tbsp balsamic vinegar

2 tbsp olive oil

A small handful of fresh thyme (or oregano) leaves, plus some small sprigs to garnish

Salt and freshly ground black pepper

1 On a lightly floured work surface, roll out the pastry to about 5mm thick. Cut out a 26cm circle, place on a baking sheet and chill for at least 30 minutes.

2 Toss the tomatoes in a bowl with the garlic, balsamic vinegar, olive oil, thyme and some salt and pepper and set them aside for a minimum of 15 minutes.

3 Preheat the oven to 220°C/fan 200°C/gas mark 7 and put a baking sheet in to heat up. Spread the marinated tomatoes over the base of your frying pan or cake tin in an even layer – they should be tightly packed.

4 Drape the pastry circle over the top, tucking it in and around the sides. Place in the oven on the hot baking sheet and bake for 25–30 minutes or until the pastry is puffy, golden and crisp. Remove and set aside for no more than 3–4 minutes.

5 Place a warmed serving plate on top of the pastry and carefully invert, then give the whole thing a firm tap or shake and remove the pan. Everything should come away cleanly and it will be all steamy and hot. Leave to cool for 30 minutes, then cut into wedges. Scatter with thyme sprigs, and serve with a green salad and a wodge of fresh bread.

winter couscous filo **TARTS**

**MAKES
6
TARTS**

EQUIPMENT
1 muffin tray or 6 x 10cm round tartlet tins

3–4 sheets of filo pastry
40g unsalted butter, melted, plus a knob for
the couscous
300g butternut squash, peeled, deseeded and
cut into 1.5cm pieces
1 red onion, cut into thin wedges
4 tbsp olive oil
1 tsp ground cumin
½ tsp smoked paprika
½ tsp dried chilli flakes
50g blanched hazelnuts, roughly chopped
100g couscous
½ x 400g tin of chickpeas, drained and rinsed
A pinch of saffron threads
200ml hot vegetable stock
Juice of 1 lemon
40g dried apricots, chopped
4 tbsp chopped fresh mint
4 tbsp chopped fresh coriander
100g feta cheese, crumbled
Salt and freshly ground black pepper

We're always on the lookout for recipes that can be prepared ahead, and this is a good example. The filo baskets can be stored in an airtight container; the couscous can sit happily in the fridge for several hours and you can throw it all together just before serving.

1 Preheat the oven to 200°C/fan 180°C/gas mark 6. Lay the sheets of filo on top of one another and slice into quarters or eighths, depending on the size of your tins. Brush one of the squares with butter and lay a second square on top. Brush that with butter and top with a third piece. You can set each piece at a different angle to make the baskets look really pretty. Repeat until you have enough filo stacks to line your tins.

2 Brush the tray or tins with a little butter and line each hole/tin with a filo stack, pressing well into the base and sides. Pop into the oven to cook for 15 minutes or until crisp and golden. Allow to cool a little so that you can handle them, then carefully remove from the tray or tins.

3 Place the squash and onion in a shallow baking tray. Add 2 tablespoons of olive oil, sprinkle in the spices and some salt, and give it all a good stir to evenly coat the vegetables. Roast in the oven for 20 minutes. Add the hazelnuts and continue to roast for a further 5 minutes.

4 Meanwhile, put the couscous into a large bowl. Stir in the chickpeas and add the saffron and remaining oil. Season with salt and pepper, then pour over the hot stock. Stir, then cover with a plate or clingfilm and set aside for 10 minutes.

5 Fluff up the couscous with a fork, then squeeze in the lemon juice, add the butter and check the seasoning. Mix in the roasted vegetables and hazelnuts, the apricots, mint, coriander and feta. Spoon the mixture into the pastry shells and serve warm.

TIP

If you've prepared the filo baskets and couscous ahead, we advise very slightly reheating them both before assembling. Place in a moderate oven for about 10–12 minutes.

smoked salmon and rocket **TARTS**

MAKES 6 TARTS

These little tarts are hard to beat. You use can use smoked salmon trimmings here; topped with a handful of rocket salad, it's a classy combination.

EQUIPMENT
6 x 10cm round fluted tartlet tins

1 quantity of Savoury Shortcrust Pastry
  (see page 212 or use ready-made pastry)
A little plain flour, for dusting

FOR THE FILLING
1 medium egg and 1 egg yolk, lightly whisked
200g crème fraîche
100ml double cream
1 tbsp hot horseradish cream
3 tbsp finely grated Gruyère cheese
130g smoked salmon
Salt and freshly ground black pepper

TO SERVE
2 tbsp extra-virgin olive oil
1 tbsp lemon juice
½ tsp Dijon mustard
70g rocket
Cracked black pepper

1 Make the savoury shortcrust pastry according to the method on page 212 and put in the fridge to rest for 30 minutes before using.

2 On a lightly floured work surface, roll out the pastry to about 2mm thick. Cut out six 15cm circles and line the tart tins with them, then prick the bases with a fork. Chill in the fridge for 30 minutes.

3 Preheat the oven to 200°C/fan 180°C/gas mark 6 and put a baking sheet in to heat up. Remove the tart tins from the fridge, line with crumpled non-stick baking paper, and fill with baking beans (see page 211). Bake in the oven on the hot baking sheet for 20 minutes, then remove the paper and beans and return to the oven for a further 5 minutes or until the base is dry and the edges are beginning to turn golden. Reduce the oven to 180°C/fan 160°C/gas mark 4.

4 Whisk the whole egg and egg yolk with the crème fraîche, double cream, horseradish and cheese. Season with a little salt and lots of black pepper. Chop the salmon into small pieces, or pulse quickly in a food processor, and stir into the egg mixture. Divide between your tart cases.

5 Place them on the hot baking sheet in the oven and bake for 30 minutes or until the filling has just set. Remove from the oven and leave to cool for 10 minutes.

6 Meanwhile, whisk together the oil, lemon juice, mustard and some salt and pepper in a large bowl. Add the rocket and gently toss to coat. Pile a handful of dressed rocket on to each tartlet, sprinkle with a little cracked black pepper and serve.

TIP

You can make the tarts in advance to the end of step 4 and keep in the fridge overnight. When ready to serve, warm them in the oven and pile the rocket salad on top.

smoked chicken and parsley pesto QUICHE

SERVES 6

The chicken adds a sweet smokiness to this quiche – but if you can't get hold of it, plain roasted chicken breast is just as delicious, especially if you add a generous grating of Parmesan to the filling.

EQUIPMENT

1 x 23cm loose-bottomed square fluted tart tin, 3cm deep

1 quantity of Savoury Shortcrust Pastry
(see page 212 or use ready-made pastry)
A little plain flour, for dusting

FOR THE FILLING

2 tbsp olive oil
1 onion, finely chopped
4 spring onions, finely sliced (white and
green parts)
200g skinless cooked smoked chicken breast,
torn into pieces
1 small bunch of fresh flat-leaf parsley, leaves
finely chopped
1 small bunch of fresh chives, snipped
Grated zest of 1 lemon
250ml double cream
3 medium eggs and 1 egg yolk, lightly whisked
2 tbsp roughly chopped hazelnuts
Salt and freshly ground black pepper
Fresh rocket leaves, to serve

1 Make the savoury shortcrust pastry according to the method on page 212 and put in the fridge to rest for 30 minutes before using.

2 On a lightly floured work surface, roll out the pastry to about 3mm thick and line your tart tin with it, making sure the edge of the pastry stands just a little proud above the rim of the tin. Trim the edges, then prick the base with a fork and return it to the fridge for a further 30 minutes. Don't be tempted to skip this step – it will help prevent shrinkage in the oven.

3 Preheat the oven to 200°C/fan 180°C/gas mark 6 and put a baking sheet in to heat up. Remove the tart tin from the fridge, line with crumpled non-stick baking paper, fill with baking beans (see page 211) and bake on the hot baking sheet in the oven for 20 minutes. Remove the paper and beans and return the tart tin to the oven for 5–8 minutes or until the base has dried out.

4 Reduce the oven to 190°C/fan 170°C/gas mark 5. Heat the oil in a frying pan over a medium heat. Cook the onion for 5 minutes to soften, then stir in the spring onions and cook for another minute. Remove to a large bowl and cool. Mix in the smoked chicken, herbs and lemon zest and spoon into your cooked pastry case. Whisk the cream and eggs together and season well with salt and pepper. Pour into the pastry case and scatter the chopped hazelnuts over the top.

5 Carefully transfer to the hot baking sheet in the oven and bake for 25–30 minutes or until the filling has just set and the pastry is golden brown. Serve warm, scattered with fresh rocket leaves.

slow-cooked french onion **TART**

**SERVES
8**

EQUIPMENT

1 x 23cm loose-bottomed round fluted tart tin

1 quantity of Savoury Shortcrust Pastry
  (see page 212 or use ready-made pastry)
A little plain flour, for dusting

FOR THE FILLING
1 tbsp olive oil
40g butter
4 large onions, sliced
2 tsp soft light brown sugar
A few sprigs of fresh thyme, leaves stripped
1 medium egg and 2 egg yolks, lightly whisked
300ml double cream
1 tbsp Dijon mustard
¼ tsp cayenne pepper
30g mature Cheddar cheese, finely grated
30g Gruyère cheese, finely grated
Salt and freshly ground black pepper

FOR THE TOPPING
A knob of butter
1 medium red onion, sliced into rings

Some combinations just work, and cheese and onion falls
neatly into that category. 'If it ain't broke, don't fix it.' So
we haven't.

1 Make the savoury shortcrust pastry according to the method on page
212 and put in the fridge to rest for 30 minutes before using.

2 On a lightly floured surface, roll out the pastry to about 3mm thick and
line your tart tin with it, making sure the edge of the pastry stands just
a little proud above the rim of the tin. Trim the edges, then prick the base
with a fork and return it to the fridge for a further 30 minutes. This is an
important step as it helps stop the pastry from shrinking in the oven.

3 Preheat the oven to 200°C/fan 180°C/gas mark 6 and put a baking
sheet in to heat up.

4 Heat the oil and butter in a large pan over a low heat. Add the onions,
season with salt and pepper and cover with a tightly fitting lid (or foil).
Cook for 30 minutes or until the onions are soft, then remove the lid,
increase the temperature and cook for 10 minutes to evaporate the liquid.
Stir in the sugar and cook for 5 minutes or until the onions start to turn
a light caramel colour. Remove to a bowl and set aside to cool. Add the
thyme leaves.

5 Meanwhile, remove the tart tin from the fridge, line with crumpled
non-stick baking paper and fill with baking beans (see page 211). Bake
in the oven on the hot baking sheet for 20 minutes. Remove the paper
and beans and return to the oven for a further 5 minutes to dry out the
base. Remove and turn the oven down to 180°C/fan 160°C/gas mark 4.

6 Scatter the onion mixture evenly into the pastry case, then whisk the whole egg and yolks with the cream, mustard, cayenne pepper, Cheddar and half the Gruyère. Pour the egg mixture over the onions and bake in the oven on the hot baking sheet for 15 minutes.

7 For the topping, melt a knob of butter in a frying pan, add the sliced red onion and cook for a minute or so over a medium heat. Cover with a lid and reduce the heat to low. Continue to cook for 3–4 minutes or until the onion is lovely and soft.

8 Remove the tart from the oven and sprinkle the softened red onion and remaining cheese over the top. Bake for a further 15 minutes or until the pastry is golden brown and the filling has set.

sweet
TREATS

red plum and ginger **TART**

**SERVES
8**

EQUIPMENT
1 x 23cm square fluted loose-bottomed tart tin

FOR THE GINGER BASE
250g ginger biscuits
50g stem ginger (3 balls)
50g butter, melted

FOR THE PLUMS
3 tbsp maple syrup
1 tbsp soft dark brown sugar
30g butter
2 sprigs of fresh thyme, plus a few extra sprigs
   for decorating
500g plums (about 8–10 depending on their size)

FOR THE FILLING
225g mascarpone
2 tbsp double cream
1 tbsp of syrup from the stem ginger jar or honey

Combining ever so slightly sweetened mascarpone with some just-baked maple-glazed plums, this tart is decadent yet surprisingly quick to make.

1 Preheat the oven to 200°C/fan 180°C/gas mark 6. Line the tart tin with non-stick baking paper to come up the sides.

2 To make the ginger base, put the biscuits with the stem ginger into a food processor and blitz until finely ground and the stem ginger has mixed into the biscuit crumbs. Add the melted butter and pulse until it is evenly combined and the biscuit mixture is beginning to clump.

3 Press the mixture firmly onto the base and up the sides of the tin to form an even layer. Place the tin on a baking sheet and bake in the oven for 5–7 minutes. Remove from the oven and leave to cool in the tin.

4 While the ginger base is baking, prepare the plums. Combine the maple syrup, sugar, butter and thyme in a small saucepan over a low heat and stir until the butter has melted and sugar has dissolved.

5 Halve and stone the plums, then place face down in an ovenproof dish and pour over the syrupy sauce. Bake in the oven for 15–20 minutes, depending on size and ripeness of the plums. The fruit should have just begun to soften. Remove from the oven and set aside.

6 In a bowl, beat the mascarpone with the cream and ginger syrup or honey until well combined.

7 Just before you are ready to serve, remove the ginger base from the tin, then top with the mascarpone mixture, spreading it just to the edge of the base. Finally, in a higgledy-piggledy manner, top with the sticky plums and carefully pour over any remaining juice. Decorate with fresh thyme.

chocolate mud pie ice cream cookie **<u>SANDWICHES</u>**

MAKES
8–10

I think there is no better way to end a meal than with a hit of something chocolatey, and this recipe for dark chocolate-chip cookies sandwiched together with ice cream is practically foolproof and surprisingly fast to make.

125g butter, softened
75g soft brown sugar
75g granulated sugar
1 medium egg
1 tsp vanilla extract
200g plain flour
35g cocoa powder
½ tsp baking powder
¼ tsp bicarbonate of soda
A pinch of salt
150g dark chocolate chips
500ml tub vanilla or chocolate ice cream
Extra chocolate, to decorate (optional)

1 In a large bowl, beat the butter and sugars together for 4 minutes until light and fluffy. Then add the egg and vanilla extract and continue to beat until evenly combined.

2 Sift the flour, cocoa powder, baking powder, bicarbonate of soda and salt together into a separate bowl. Stir the flour mixture into the egg mixture, then stir in the chocolate chips. Bring the mixture together to form a firm dough. Divide the dough into 20 small pieces (30g each) and shape each into a disc. Put on a baking tray lined with non-stick baking paper, cover with clingfilm and chill in the fridge for at least 2 hours.

3 Preheat the oven to 180°C/fan 160°/gas mark 4.

4 Bake the cookies in the oven for 8–10 minutes. Remove from the oven and leave to firm up on the tray for 10 minutes before transferring to a wire rack to cool completely.

5 Working quickly, scoop the ice cream onto one cookie and sandwich it together with another cookie. Return each complete cookie sandwich to the freezer until they have all been assembled. Serve immediately or leave in the freezer for serving later.

6 If you like, melt a little extra chocolate in a small bowl over simmering water and drizzle over the sandwiches when serving.

salted pecan fudge **PIE**

This is a real classic: pastry, toasted pecans, brown sugar and cream. You can eat it cold, but it's best served straight from the oven with a large scoop of vanilla ice cream.

EQUIPMENT
1 x 23cm loose-bottomed round fluted tart tin

1 quantity of Sweet Shortcrust Pastry
  (see page 215)
A little plain flour, for dusting
100g pecan nuts, chopped, plus 80–100g
  pecan halves
100g soft light brown sugar
125g butter
200ml double cream
1 tsp salt, ideally good-quality salt such as
  fleur de sel
2 medium eggs, beaten
3 tbsp apricot jam, warmed
Whipped cream or vanilla ice cream, to serve

1 Make the sweet shortcrust pastry according to the method on page 215 and put in the fridge to rest for 30 minutes.

2 On a lightly floured work surface, roll out your pastry to about 3mm thick and line your tart tin with it, making sure the edge of the pastry stands just a little proud above the rim. Trim the edges, prick the base with a fork and return it to the fridge for a further 30 minutes. Don't miss this step – it helps stop the pastry shrinking in the oven.

3 Preheat the oven to 200°C/fan 180°C/gas mark 6 and put a baking sheet in to heat up. Remove the tin from the fridge, line with crumpled non-stick baking paper and fill with baking beans (see page 211). Bake in the oven on the hot baking sheet for 20 minutes, then remove the paper and beans and continue to cook for 5–10 minutes or until the pastry is dry. Set aside.

4 Spread the chopped pecans evenly over a baking sheet (reserve the pecan halves for later) and lightly toast in the oven for 8–10 minutes, making sure they don't burn. Set aside to cool. Reduce the oven to 180°C/fan 160°C/gas mark 4.

5 Place the sugar, butter and cream in a pan and cook over a low heat, stirring constantly, until the sugar has completely dissolved. Cool slightly, then stir in the cooled toasted nuts, salt and beaten eggs. Pour the mixture into the pastry case. Arrange the reserved pecan halves over the top of the pie in a circular pattern. Bake in the oven on the hot baking sheet for 25 minutes.

6 Take the pie out of the oven and let it cool a little, then brush the top with the warmed apricot jam. This pie is nice served just warm, with whipped cream or vanilla ice cream.

tart lemon
TART

SERVES
8

EQUIPMENT
1 x 21cm loose-bottomed round fluted tart tin

1 quantity of Sweet Shortcrust Pastry, with the
    addition of the grated zest of 1 orange and
    1 lemon (see pages 213 and 215)
A little plain flour, for dusting
3 tbsp berry jam, warmed
5 medium eggs
25g butter, melted
Juice and grated zest of 3 large unwaxed lemons
    (about 175ml juice)
150g caster sugar
Icing sugar, for dusting
Pouring cream, to serve

It didn't take me long to learn that my husband James has a serious 'sour' addiction: he loves grapefruit, lime, lemon and vinegar. Anything sharp tends to be his pudding choice, so I've perfected his favourite tart to make him smile. Forgive me if it is a little too 'tart' for you – it's just the way he likes it.

1 Make the sweet shortcrust pastry according to the method on pages 213 and 215, adding the orange and lemon zest, and put it in the fridge to rest for 30 minutes before using.

2 On a lightly floured work surface, roll out the pastry to about 3mm thick and line your tart tin with it, making sure the edge of the pastry stands just a little proud above the rim. Trim the edges, prick the base with a fork and return it to the fridge for a further 30 minutes. Don't be tempted to skip this step – it helps stop the pastry shrinking while cooking.

3 Preheat the oven to 200°C/fan 180°C/gas mark 6 and put a baking sheet in to heat up. Remove the tin from the fridge, line with crumpled non-stick baking paper and fill with baking beans (see page 211). Bake on the hot baking sheet for 20 minutes, then remove the paper and beans and return to the oven for 5 minutes or until the pastry is dry. Set aside to cool a little.

4 Reduce the oven to 150°C/fan 130°C/gas mark 2. Spread the jam over the base of the pastry case, using the back of the spoon to get it all nicely level.

5 In a large bowl, lightly beat the eggs, then add the melted butter, lemon zest, juice and caster sugar. Stir well, then pour into the jammy pastry case and bake on the hot baking sheet for 30 minutes or until the filling has just set. Allow to cool slightly, then remove from the tin.

6 Allow to cool completely, then add a heavy dusting of icing sugar. Serve in thin slices, with a puddle of cream.

TIP

Don't worry if it seems like there is too much filling – it will sink while cooking.

key lime **PIE**
with lime jelly

EQUIPMENT

1 x 23cm loose-bottomed round fluted tart tin

1 quantity of Sweet Shortcrust Pastry, with the
   addition of 1 tbsp ground ginger (see pages
   213 and 215)
4 medium egg yolks
1 x 400g tin of condensed milk
Juice of 4 limes (140ml) and grated zest of 2 limes

FOR THE JELLY
3 sheets of gelatine
Juice of 5 limes (175ml) and grated zest of 1 lime
40g caster sugar
1 drop of green food colouring

FOR THE GINGER CREAM
300ml double cream
2 tbsp ginger syrup (from a jar of stem ginger)
1 ball of stem ginger, chopped

I've spent long parts of my career living and working in Seattle. It is a city I love and where I've tasted some of the best key lime pies (even though the recipe originally comes from the Florida Keys). The important thing for this pie is that the filling combines creaminess with a really good citrus kick.

1 Make the sweet shortcrust pastry according to the method on page 215, adding the ground ginger (see page 213), and put it into the fridge to rest for 30 minutes before using.

2 Roll out the pastry to about 3mm thick and line your tart tin with it, making sure the edge of the pastry stands just a little proud above the rim. Trim the edges, prick the base with a fork and return to the fridge for 30 minutes. This helps to stop the pastry from shrinking – so don't skip this step.

3 Preheat the oven to 200°C/fan 180°C/gas mark 6 and put a baking sheet in to heat up. Remove your pastry case from the fridge, line with crumpled non-stick baking paper and fill with baking beans (see page 211). Bake in the oven on the hot baking sheet for 20 minutes, then remove the baking paper and beans and return to the oven for a further 5 minutes or until the pastry is dry. Remove and set aside. Reduce the oven to 180°C/fan 160°C/gas mark 4.

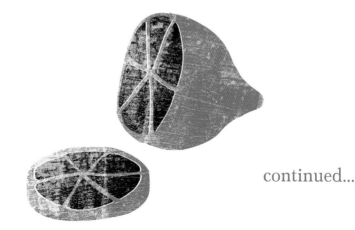

continued...

key lime **PIE**
with lime jelly
continued...

4 Beat the egg yolks in a large bowl with an electric whisk for 3 minutes. Add the condensed milk and continue to whisk for a couple of minutes. Finally, whisk in the lime juice and zest. Spoon the mixture over the pastry base, swirling it with the back of a spoon to cover evenly. Bake in the oven on the hot baking sheet for 15–20 minutes or until just set. Remove and allow to cool completely, then remove from the tin and chill in the fridge.

5 For the lime jelly, soak the gelatine sheets in cold water for 5 minutes. Put the lime juice, 60ml of water and the caster sugar into a saucepan and slowly bring almost to the boil, to dissolve the sugar. Remove from the heat. Squeeze the excess water from the gelatine sheets and add them to the pan. Stir to dissolve. Add the lime zest and colouring, stir, then transfer to a jug and leave to cool for 30 minutes.

6 Pour the jelly over the top of the pie, stopping when you fear it might dribble over the sides. Return to the fridge for 1 hour to set. Combine the cream and ginger syrup in a mixing bowl and whisk to soft peaks, then stir in the chopped stem ginger and serve with slices of the finished pie.

pear and whisky TART

SERVES
6

EQUIPMENT

1 loose-bottomed fluted rectangular tin, 36cm x 12cm x 3cm

1 quantity of Sweet Shortcrust Pastry
   (see page 215)
A little plain flour, for dusting
6 dumpy, ripe pears
3 tbsp caster sugar
Pouring cream, to serve

FOR THE FRANGIPANE FILLING
75g butter, softened
75g light brown muscovado sugar
75g ground almonds
50g self-raising flour, sifted
2 medium eggs, beaten
Grated zest and juice of 1 large orange

FOR THE GLAZE
2 tbsp whisky
3 tbsp marmalade, with bits

At some point during December, I find I'm through with mincemeat. This tart is perfect to pull out at those moments, when we still want a bit of warmth from our puddings. The snap of whisky and the dumpy pears nestled in frangipane are just the thing to cheer up a dark winter's day.

1 Make the sweet shortcrust pastry according to the method on page 215 and put it into the fridge to rest for 30 minutes.

2 On a lightly floured work surface, roll out the pastry to about 3mm thick, then drape it over your tin, pressing it well into the sides with your fingers. Roll your rolling pin over the top to remove the excess pastry, then put the uncooked pastry case into the fridge to rest for at least 30 minutes.

3 Carefully peel the pears, removing all the skin but leaving the stalks intact. Slice off the bottoms so that the pears will sit upright on a flat surface. Heat 1 litre water in a large saucepan, stir in the caster sugar and bring to a simmer. Gently lower the pears into the liquid and poach them for 20 minutes or until just soft. Remove with a slotted spoon and set aside to cool.

4 Meanwhile, make the frangipane filling. Using an electric whisk or a wooden spoon and a firm wrist, beat the butter, sugar, ground almonds, flour, eggs and orange zest with half the orange juice until smooth and creamy.

continued...

pear and whisky **TART**
continued...

5 Preheat the oven to 200°C/fan 180°C/gas mark 6 and put a baking sheet in to heat up. Remove your pastry base from the fridge and line up the poached pears in a row along the bottom. Using a large spoon, dollop the frangipane around the pears and gently press into the corners using the back of a smaller spoon.

6 Place the tart on the hot baking sheet in the preheated oven and bake for 30 minutes or until the filling is just firm to the touch. Remove from the oven and set aside to cool.

7 For an elegant finish, strain the remaining orange juice into a small pan and add the whisky and marmalade. Stir over a low heat until just warm and any lumps of marmalade have melted. Using a pastry brush, dab this glaze all over the tart, allowing the liquid to seep into any cracks. That's it – serve in slices with a jug of cold cream.

rhubarb crumble
TARTS

EQUIPMENT
6 x 10cm round fluted tartlet tins

1 quantity of Sweet Shortcrust Pastry
  (see page 215)
A little plain flour, for dusting
600g rhubarb (the pinker the better!), cut into
  2.5 cm pieces
120g caster sugar
Juice and grated zest of ½ an orange

FOR THE CRUMBLE
25g plain flour
30g soft light brown sugar
25g rolled oats
35g butter, chilled and diced

FOR THE FILLING
120g mascarpone
2 tbsp icing sugar
200ml double cream
½ tsp vanilla bean paste

Rhubarb crumble is a classic for good reason. Sharp rhubarb contrasts perfectly in taste and texture with sweet crumble. Here we have combined them into little tarts that are bound to impress your guests.

1 Make the sweet shortcrust pastry according to the method on page 215 and put it in the fridge to rest for 30 minutes.

2 On a lightly floured work surface, roll out the pastry to about 2mm thick. Cut out six 15cm circles, line the tins with them and prick the bases with a fork. Chill for 30 minutes.

3 Preheat the oven to 200°C/fan 180°C/gas mark 6 and put a baking sheet in to heat up. Line each tartlet case with non-stick baking paper and fill with baking beans (see page 211). Bake on the hot baking sheet in the oven for 15 minutes, then remove the paper and beans and continue to cook for 5–10 minutes or until the pastry is dry. Cool and remove from the tins. Reduce the oven to 180°C/fan 160°C/gas mark 4.

4 Toss the rhubarb in a bowl with the sugar, orange zest and juice. Spread over a shallow baking tray and bake for 20 minutes or until tender. Tip into a bowl and allow to cool.

5 For the crumble, mix the flour, sugar and oats in a bowl. Rub the butter in with your fingertips until you have coarse crumbs. Scatter over a baking sheet lined with non-stick baking paper and bake for 18–20 minutes or until golden. Break up with a wooden spoon if needed. Set aside to cool.

6 To make the filling, whip the mascarpone to loosen it, then add the sugar, cream and vanilla paste and whip until smooth. Divide between your tartlet cases, smoothing with the back of a spoon. Add the rhubarb and finish with the crumble topping. Drizzle over a little rhubarb juice to serve.

mincemeat and apple christmas CROUSTADE

SERVES
8

Think of this recipe as a giant mince pie to be shared. We've made our own mincemeat, loaded with citrusy zest and juice, but you can replace with 550g of shop-bought mincemeat, which can be almost as good.

200g plain flour, sifted, plus a little for dusting

A pinch of salt

125g butter, chilled and diced, plus a little melted butter for brushing

3 tbsp caster sugar

1 medium egg, lightly beaten, plus extra for brushing

30g ground almonds

2 small Bramley apples or 1 large one, peeled, cored and cut into chunks

2 small Cox's apples, peeled, cored and finely sliced

Brandy cream or brandy butter, to serve

FOR THE MINCEMEAT (MAKES 550G)

1 Bramley apple, peeled, cored and coarsely grated

Juice and grated zest of 1 orange

Juice and grated zest of 1 lemon

70g dried cranberries

30g flaked almonds

200g sultanas

40g suet

100g soft light brown sugar

2 tsp mixed spice

1 tbsp brandy (optional)

1 A few hours or a day before you want to make the croustade, mix all the mincemeat ingredients together and set aside, covered, to allow the flavours to develop.

2 To make the pastry, mix the flour and salt in a large bowl, or pulse in a food processor for a couple of seconds, then add the butter and rub in with your fingertips or pulse until you have fine crumbs. Mix in 2 tablespoons of sugar, then add the egg and mix with a round-bladed knife or pulse until the mixture just starts to form large clumps. Tip on to a lightly floured work surface and knead briefly with your hands. Shape into a flat disc, wrap in clingfilm and chill for 30 minutes.

3 Preheat the oven to 200°C/fan 180°C/gas mark 6. Line a baking sheet with non-stick baking paper. On a lightly floured work surface, roll out the pastry to a 36cm circle, about 3mm thick. Sprinkle with the ground almonds, then transfer to the lined baking sheet.

4 Mix the Bramley apple chunks with the mincemeat and spoon into the middle of the waiting pastry. Arrange the Cox's apple slices in an overlapping circle in the centre, and bring up the sides of the pastry to enclose the filling, leaving the apple slices exposed.

5 Brush the pastry with beaten egg and the apple slices with melted butter. Sprinkle both with the remaining caster sugar. Bake for 40–45 minutes or until the pastry is crisp and the filling is cooked and tender. Serve hot with brandy cream or brandy butter.

TIP

You can make the mincemeat in advance (up to 3 months) and store in a sealed jar in the fridge.

cranberry and orange gluten-free mince **PIES**

MAKES
12
PIES

EQUIPMENT
1 x shallow bun tin; 1 x 8cm round plain or fluted and 1 x star-shaped pastry cutter

1 quantity of Gluten-free Shortcrust Pastry
  (see page 216 and step 1 of the method)
Grated zest of 1 orange, plus a little extra (optional)
  for the filling
A little gluten-free flour, for dusting

FOR THE FILLING
250g gluten-free mincemeat
55g dried cranberries

FOR THE MONT BLANC EFFECT
150ml double cream
1 heaped tbsp icing sugar
Freeze-dried raspberry powder, for sprinkling
Zest of 1 orange or blood orange

I really do feel for my gluten-free friends. Life without mince pies… well, I wouldn't wish that on anybody. With that in mind, I've developed a way to make a very good sweet pastry without using wheat flour. In fact these mince pies, with their Christmassy topping of whipped cream and raspberry dust, will bring pleasure to all, not just the pastry-deprived.

1 Make the gluten-free pastry according to the method on page 216, adding the orange zest at the end of step 1 and then following the recipe to the end.

2 On a lightly floured work surface, roll out the pastry to about 2mm thick. Cut out twelve 8cm plain or fluted circles using the round pastry cutter and press the pastry gently into the holes of the bun tin. Return to the fridge to chill for 30 minutes. Cut out twelve stars using the star-shaped cutter from the remaining pastry and place on a baking sheet lined with non-stick baking paper.

3 Preheat the oven to 190°C/fan 170°C/gas mark 5. For the filling, measure the mincemeat into a bowl and stir in the dried cranberries, along with a little orange zest to zhoosh up your mincemeat, if you like. Spoon the mincemeat mixture into the pastry cases – it should reach about three-quarters of the way up the sides.

4 Place the mince pies on the middle shelf of the oven and the pastry stars on the shelf below. Bake the stars for about 12 minutes or until golden brown, and bake the mince pies for 25 minutes or until the pastry is golden. Allow the pies to cool completely before removing from the bun tin.

5 Using an electric whisk, whip the double cream with the icing sugar in a large bowl until it just forms soft peaks. Top each cooled mince pie with a generous dollop of the whipped cream, sprinkle with freeze-dried raspberry powder and orange zest and push a pastry star into the cream. Serve immediately.

jumble berry
TART

EQUIPMENT
1 x 23cm loose-bottomed round fluted tart tin

1 quantity of Sweet Shortcrust Pastry
  (see page 215)
A little plain flour, for dusting
75g butter, softened
75g caster sugar
75g ground almonds
50g self-raising flour
2 medium eggs, beaten
Juice and grated zest of 1 large orange
4 tbsp berry jam, e.g. raspberry or woodland
200g frozen berries, e.g. blackberries, blueberries,
  raspberries, strawberries, redcurrants
15g almonds, cut into slivers (ones with skins
  look prettiest)
2 tbsp apricot jam, warmed
Thick double cream or crème fraîche, to serve

This gorgeous tart is oozing with jam, sharp berries and fudgy almonds, all jumbled on top of delicious crisp pastry. It's great for just about any day of the year.

1 Make the sweet shortcrust pastry according to the method on page 215 and put it into the fridge to rest for 30 minutes.

2 On a lightly floured work surface, roll out your pastry to about 3mm thick, then drape it over your tart tin, pressing it well into the sides with your fingers. Roll your rolling pin over the top to remove the excess pastry. Chill the lined tart case for at least 30 minutes.

3 Meanwhile, make the frangipane for the filling. Using an electric whisk or a wooden spoon and a firm wrist, beat the butter, sugar, almonds, flour, eggs and orange juice and zest until smooth and creamy.

4 Preheat the oven to 200°C/180°C/gas mark 6 and put a baking sheet in to heat up. Remove the tart tin from the fridge and spread 2 tablespoons of jam over the pastry base. Using a large spoon, dollop the frangipane on top of the jam, spreading it evenly across the base. Toss the frozen berries in the remaining jam and sprinkle over the frangipane. Sprinkle with the slivered almonds.

5 Place the tart on the hot baking sheet in the oven and bake for 30 minutes or until the filling is just firm to the touch. If it needs a few minutes longer, reduce the oven temperature to 180°C/fan 160°C/gas mark 4. Remove the tart from the oven and set aside to cool for 30 minutes.

6 Brush the warm apricot jam all over the tart and serve warm or cold, cut into wedges, with dollops of thick double cream or crème fraîche.

honeyed nut and custard **TART**

SERVES 8

EQUIPMENT
1 x 23cm loose-bottomed round fluted tart tin

FOR THE PASTRY
185g plain flour, plus a little for dusting
55g icing sugar
30g ground almonds
A pinch of salt
125g butter, chilled and cubed
1 medium egg yolk, beaten
Approx. 1 tbsp ice-cold water

FOR THE HONEY CUSTARD
200ml double cream
2 eggs, lightly whisked
100g caster sugar
2 tbsp runny honey
1 tsp vanilla extract

FOR THE NUT TOPPING
2 tbsp runny honey, plus more for brushing,
   if you like
A knob or two of butter
50g shelled pistachios, roughly chopped
50 walnuts, roughly chopped
50g hazelnuts, toasted and roughly chopped

The generous scattering of honeyed nuts on this tart is inspired by Greek baklava and sandy beaches in the sun.

1 Start by making the pastry. Sift the flour, icing sugar, ground almonds and salt into a large bowl. Rub the butter into the mixture with your fingertips until it resembles breadcrumbs (or pulse in a food processor).

2 Add the beaten egg yolk and just enough of the water to bring the mixture together, mixing with a round-bladed knife. Knead very briefly with your hands, then shape into a disc, wrap in clingfilm and chill in the fridge for 30 minutes.

3 On a lightly floured work surface, roll out the pastry to about 3mm thick and line your tart tin with it, making sure the edge of the pastry stands just a little proud above the rim. Trim the edges, prick the base with a fork and return it to the fridge for a further 30 minutes. Don't be tempted to skip this step – it helps to stop the pastry shrinking as it cooks.

4 Preheat the oven to 200°C/fan 180°C/gas mark 6 and put a baking sheet in to heat up. Take your pastry case from the fridge, line with crumpled non-stick baking paper and fill with baking beans (see page 211). Place on the hot baking sheet in the oven and bake for 20 minutes, then remove the paper and beans and return to the oven for a further 5 minutes. Remove from the oven and set aside.

continued...

honeyed nut and custard **TART**
continued...

5 Reduce the oven to 180°C/fan 160°C/gas mark 4. Leave the hot baking sheet inside.

6 To make the honey custard, heat the cream in a saucepan over a medium heat and bring almost to the boil. In a separate bowl, mix together the eggs, sugar, honey and vanilla extract until amalgamated. Slowly pour in the hot cream and stir well until incorporated. Try not to beat any air into the mixture – you want it to be as smooth as possible.

7 Gently pour the custard into the cooled tart case and bake on the hot baking sheet in the oven for 30 minutes or until the custard is set but not coloured. Remove from the oven.

8 The nut topping is very quick to prepare and makes the tart look fabulous. Heat the honey and a knob of butter in a small frying pan over a high heat. Throw in the nuts and coat in the buttery honey. Heat for a further 2 minutes, then tip out onto your tart and serve. Drizzle or brush with more melted butter and honey if you like it sweet.

oaty treacle
TART

EQUIPMENT
1 x 23cm loose-bottomed square tart tin

1 quantity of Sweet Shortcrust Pastry
   (see page 215)
A little plain flour, for dusting

FOR THE FILLING
300g golden syrup
220ml double cream
2 medium eggs, lightly whisked
100g rolled oats
Finely grated zest of 1 lemon

Amy, who does the marketing at Higgidy, says this is the best treacle tart she's ever eaten: 'all fudgy, with a lemony kick'.

1 Make the sweet shortcrust pastry according to the method on page 215 and put it into the fridge to rest for 30 minutes.

2 On a lightly floured work surface, roll out your pastry to about 3mm thick and line your tart tin with it, making sure the edge of the pastry stands just a little proud above the rim. Trim the edges, prick the base with a fork and return it to the fridge for a further 30 minutes. This is an important step as it helps to stop the pastry shrinking in the oven.

3 Preheat the oven to 200°C/fan 180°C/gas mark 6 and put a baking sheet in to heat up. Remove your pastry case from the fridge, line with crumpled non-stick baking paper and fill with baking beans (see page 211). Bake in the oven on the baking sheet for 20 minutes, then remove the baking paper and beans and return to the oven for a further 5 minutes or until the pastry is dry. Remove and set aside. Reduce the oven to 180°C/fan 160°C/gas mark 4.

4 Warm the golden syrup in a pan over a gentle heat until tiny bubbles appear, then remove from the heat. In a medium bowl, mix the cream and eggs. Add the oats and lemon zest, and stir to combine. Lastly, pour in the warm syrup and give the whole lot a good stir with a wooden spoon. Pour into the baked pastry case.

5 Bake the tart on the hot baking sheet in the oven for about 30 minutes or until the pastry is crisp and golden and the filling feels set in the middle when gently pressed. Cool in the tin for 10–15 minutes, then remove from the tin and serve just a little bit warm.

chocolate
snowflake **TART**

EQUIPMENT

1 x 23cm loose-bottomed round fluted tart tin; snowflake stencil (see recipe introduction)

1 quantity of Chocolate Shortcrust Pastry
  (see page 215)
A little plain flour, for dusting
300ml double cream
300g light muscovado sugar
300g dark chocolate, (at least 70% cocoa solids),
  broken into pieces
Icing sugar, for decorating

However organised I try to be in the run-up to Christmas, I always feel on the back foot. This pudding can be made ahead and stuck in the freezer. Leave to thaw overnight and simply decorate on the day. Snowflake stencils are available online or you can make your own by cutting snowflake shapes from paper. Alternatively, simply pop a sprig of holly on top.

1 Make the chocolate shortcrust pastry according to the method on page 215 and put it into the fridge to rest for 30 minutes before using.

2 On a lightly floured work surface, roll out the pastry to about 3mm thick and line the tart tin with it. Trim the edges, prick the base with a fork and chill for a further 30 minutes.

3 Preheat the oven to 200°C/fan 180°C/gas mark 6 and put a baking sheet in to heat up. Remove the tin from the fridge, line with crumpled non-stick baking paper and fill with baking beans (see page 211). Place in the oven on the hot baking sheet and bake for 20 minutes, then remove the paper and beans and return to the oven for 8–10 minutes or until dry and cooked through. Remove from the tin and leave to cool completely.

4 To make the filling, put the cream and muscovado sugar into a saucepan and heat gently until the sugar has dissolved. Add the chocolate and continue to stir over a low heat until it has melted and the mixture is beautifully smooth. Pour the filling into the cooled pastry case and leave to set in the fridge for at least 2 hours.

5 Rest your snowflake stencil on top of your tart. Using a light hand, gently sprinkle icing sugar over the top, then remove your stencil to unveil the decorations. Serve with festive cheer.

apple and blackberry **PIE**

SERVES
8

EQUIPMENT
1 x 18–20cm round ovenproof pie dish;
pie funnel (optional)

FOR THE PASTRY
250g plain flour, plus a little for dusting
A pinch of salt
½ tsp ground cinnamon
250g butter, chilled and diced
2–3 tbsp ice-cold water
1 medium egg, lightly beaten

FOR THE FILLING
600g Bramley apples, peeled, cored and roughly
    chopped (about 6 medium apples)
1 tbsp lemon juice
40g soft light brown sugar
2 tbsp cornflour
150g fresh blackberries

FOR THE TOPPING
¼ tsp ground cinnamon
1 tbsp golden caster sugar

Surely it's no coincidence that these two beautiful fruits ripen at the same time? In September, my children Kate and Jack like to go blackberry picking. They trot off with bowls in hand and return with stained fingers (and often school uniforms!). I let them don a little apron each to help me make the pastry. If you follow suit, be prepared to have a flour-dusted kitchen.

1 Sift the flour, salt and cinnamon into a large bowl and stir. Add the butter and mix with a round-bladed knife until the mixture resembles small breadcrumbs (or pulse in a food processor). Add the water and quickly mix in, using the knife rather than your hands, until it starts to form large clumps (add a little more water if needed). Now use your hands to bring the dough together, then knead briefly and form into a disc. Wrap in clingfilm and chill for 30 minutes.

2 On a lightly floured work surface, roll out the pastry to a large rectangle (approx. 40cm x 25cm). With the shorter side towards you, fold the top third down to the centre and the bottom third up. Then fold in half to create a neat, square parcel. Give the pastry a quarter turn. Roll out once again to a large rectangle and repeat the folding. Wrap in clingfilm and chill again for at least 30 minutes. Overnight is best.

3 Preheat the oven to 200°C/fan 180°C/gas mark 6. On a lightly floured work surface, roll out the pastry to about 3mm thick. Use a little more than half of it to line your pie dish, and brush with beaten egg. Use the remaining pastry to create a lid: roll a circle about 5cm wider than the diameter of your pie dish and set aside.

continued...

apple and
blackberry **PIE**
continued...

4 In a large bowl, gently toss the apple chunks with the lemon juice, brown sugar, cornflour and blackberries. Pile the fruit into your pastry-lined pie dish, heaping it up in the middle. Add a pie funnel, if using. Gently cover with the prepared pastry lid, cutting a funnel hole if needed. Press (don't stretch) the pastry against the fruit and the bottom crust. With a sharp knife, trim the dough flush to the dish and crimp the edges (see page 210).

5 Unless you've added a pie funnel, cut three or four vents in the lid to let steam escape, and decorate with shapes cut from leftover pastry, rolled to about 2mm thick. Brush with beaten egg and sprinkle on the cinnamon and sugar for the topping.

6 Bake on the centre shelf of the oven for 30 minutes, then reduce the oven to 160°C/fan 140°C/gas mark 3 and cook for a further 15 minutes or until you can see juices bubbling through the steam vents or inside the funnel. Allow to cool before serving.

bright red jam **TARTS**

MAKES
18
TARTS

EQUIPMENT
2 shallow bun tins;
1 x 7cm round pastry cutter

1 quantity of Sweet Shortcrust Pastry
  (see page 215)
A little plain flour, for dusting
6 tbsp raspberry jam, or about ½ a pot
150g fresh raspberries

My beautiful eleven-year-old daughter, Kate, seems to have
inherited my love of all things food-related. When asked
'How was school today?' her stock response is to simply
recall the lunch menu. Together the two of us made this
recipe, with Kate squashing the raspberries into the jam.
We had so much fun that we had to include it in this book.

1 Make the sweet shortcrust pastry according to the method on page
215 and put it in the fridge to rest for 30 minutes.

2 On a lightly floured work surface, roll out the pastry to about 2mm
thick. Cut out about eighteen 7cm circles and line the holes in the bun
tins. Return to the fridge to chill for 30 minutes.

3 Preheat the oven to 190°C/fan 170°C/gas mark 5. When you are
ready to fill the tarts, spoon a little jam into each pastry case – it should
reach about three-quarters of the way up the sides. Add a raspberry or
two to each case and submerge in the jam. It doesn't matter if a little
fruit pokes out – it makes the tarts all the more beautiful.

4 Bake in the oven for 25 minutes or until the pastry has turned golden.
Be very careful when you take the tarts out of the oven, as the jam will
be very hot. Allow to cool for 30 minutes and serve – if you can wait
that long!

white chocolate
TARTS

**MAKES
6
TARTS**

EQUIPMENT
6 x 10cm round tartlet tins

1 quantity of Sweet Shortcrust Pastry
  (see page 215)
A little plain flour, for dusting
Edible rose petals, to decorate

FOR THE FILLING
175g good-quality white chocolate, broken up
150ml soured cream
150ml double cream

If you're careful melting the white chocolate, these are very easy and can be prepared up to 8 hours ahead. If you can't get rose petals, try just dusting the top heavily with cocoa powder.

1 Make the sweet shortcrust pastry according to the method on page 215 and put it in the fridge to rest for 30 minutes.

2 On a lightly floured work surface, roll out your pastry to about 2mm thick and cut out six 15cm circles. Carefully line the tins with them, trimming any excess, and put in the fridge for 30 minutes – this helps prevent shrinkage in the oven.

3 Preheat the oven to 200°C/fan 180°C/gas mark 6 and put a baking sheet in to heat up. Line each case with non-stick baking paper and fill with baking beans (see page 211). Place on the hot baking sheet in the oven and bake for 15 minutes, then remove the beans and paper and return to the oven for 8–10 minutes or until the pastry feels dry to the touch. Leave to cool completely.

4 Melt the chocolate in a heatproof bowl set over a pan of hot but not boiling water. Once melted, remove from the heat and stir in the soured cream. In a separate bowl, whip the double cream until it just forms soft peaks, then mix it gently into the white chocolate mixture. Spoon into the pastry cases and allow to set for at least 2 hours in the fridge. Decorate with rose petals to serve.

raspberry almond
PITHIVIER

SERVES
8

I'm all for being a bit crafty in the kitchen. There are times when making everything from scratch is hugely rewarding. But sometimes a bit of judicious corner cutting can yield equally good results in a fraction of the time. This recipe, with its ready-made puff pastry, raspberry jam and marzipan, is as easy as it is impressive.

500g all-butter puff pastry
A little plain flour, for dusting
100g white marzipan
100g ground almonds
45ml double cream
2 medium eggs, beaten, plus a beaten egg
    for glazing
4 tbsp good-quality raspberry jam
A dozen or so fresh raspberries
Soft brown sugar, for dusting

1 Preheat the oven to 220°C/425°F/gas mark 7. Line a baking tray with non-stick baking paper. Cut the puff pastry block into two equal pieces. On a lightly floured work surface, roll out each of the puff pastry pieces into circles measuring about 25cm in diameter. Place one pastry circle on the baking tray.

2 Grate the marzipan into a bowl, then add the ground almonds, cream and eggs. Mix until evenly combined.

3 Spread the jam over the base of one pastry circle, leaving a border 2cm wide around the edge. Squish the fresh raspberries into the jam and carefully spread the marzipan mixture evenly over the jammy base.

4 Brush the edge of the pastry with some of the beaten egg and then top with the second pastry circle. Seal all around the edge by gently pressing with a fork. Make some tiny holes in the upper crust to allow steam to escape and then, using a sharp knife, make a pattern on the top of the pastry. Brush with the beaten egg and dust with a sprinkling of soft brown sugar.

5 Bake the pithivier in the oven for 20 to 25 minutes or until puffed up and golden. Set aside to cool for at least 30 minutes before cutting into wedges and serving.

sticky ginger and apple
TARTE TATIN

**SERVES
8**

Tarte Tatin turns apple pie on its head! It's really not as complicated as you might think. We make ours in a cake tin rather than a pan, which we find works perfectly.

EQUIPMENT

1 x 20cm fixed-based round cake tin

A little plain flour, for dusting

500g all-butter puff pastry

50g unsalted butter

100g soft dark brown sugar

3 balls of stem ginger, very finely chopped (approx. 40g)

2 tbsp ginger syrup (from the stem ginger jar)

600g Granny Smith apples, peeled, cored and cut in half (3–4 apples)

Thick double cream, to serve

1 Preheat the oven to 220°C/fan 200°C/gas mark 7.

2 On a lightly floured work surface, roll out the pastry to about 5mm thick. Place your cake tin on top of the pastry and cut out a circle around it, allowing a 1–2cm border of excess pastry around the tin. Place your pastry circle on a baking sheet in the fridge.

3 Melt the butter in a small frying pan over a medium heat, then add the sugar and stir to break up any lumps. Add the stem ginger and ginger syrup. Shake the pan gently but do not stir, and allow to bubble for a minute. Pour this caramel into the bottom of your cake tin.

4 Arrange the apples, rounded sides facing the bottom of the tin, on top of the caramel. Squeeze in as many halves you can – any raised edges will sort themselves out in the oven. Cover with your prepared pastry circle, tucking the edges inside the tin around the apples.

5 Place in the oven and bake for 30 minutes or until the pastry is golden brown and puffed up.

6 Remove from the oven and leave to cool for 15–20 minutes, then hold a serving plate tightly over the tin and flip them both over as fast as you can. Serve warm, in slices, with thick double cream.

TIP

This pudding can be assembled 4–6 hours in advance. Once the caramel and apples are tucked carefully under the pastry, just pop the tin in the fridge until you're ready to bake.

christmas cranberry **CRACKERS**

MAKES
12
CRACKERS

These crackers were inspired by my son Jack, who was born post-Christmas but pre-New Year, so he gets his own celebration before the tree has been taken down. You can vary the recipe as you wish – try adding spices, ginger, raisins or apricots.

1 x 270g pack of filo pastry
50g butter, melted

FOR THE FILLING
60g dried cranberries
Juice and finely grated zest of 1 large orange
100g cream cheese
50g ground almonds
1 egg yolk
25g icing sugar, plus extra for dusting

1 Begin by soaking your cranberries in the fresh orange juice for 30 minutes. This will plump them up nicely.

2 Strain the cranberries and place in a large bowl, discarding any remaining juice. Add the rest of the filling ingredients and give the mixture a good stir. Chill for a minimum of 30 minutes before using.

3 When you are ready to assemble the crackers, preheat the oven to 180°C/fan 160°C/gas mark 4. Cut the stack of filo into 11cm x 18cm rectangles. Brush one filo rectangle with melted butter and top with a second piece of filo.

4 Dollop a good teaspoonful of filling into the centre of this rectangle and brush around the filling with a little more melted butter. Then wrap it up as if you were wrapping a sweet (not too tightly, as the filling will expand while cooking and burst the seams), squeezing the pastry together about 3cm in from each edge. Continue until all the filling and pastry is used up.

5 Arrange on a baking tray lined with non-stick baking paper, brush with a little more butter and bake for 15–20 minutes or until the filo is crispy and golden. Finish with a light dusting of icing sugar.

TIP
For adults it's fun to serve these with little cups of espresso, or even a lightly sweetened whisky cream for indulgent dipping.

elderflower and raspberry
BAKED APPLES

SERVES
6

A quick apple pie that has been scaled down, for those self-indulgent moments.

EQUIPMENT
1 x 8cm round fluted pastry cutter

A little plain flour, for dusting
320g ready-rolled all-butter puff pastry
100g fresh raspberries
120g good-quality raspberry jam
6 eating apples, Granny Smith or Cox's
100ml elderflower cordial
A knob of butter
1 medium egg, beaten
1–2 tbsp caster sugar
Vanilla ice cream, to serve

1 Preheat the oven to 200°C/fan 180°C/gas mark 6. Unroll the pastry on to a lightly floured work surface and cut out six circles with the cutter. Using the remaining pastry, cut out some little leaves and 'stalks' to decorate the pastry hats. Set these all aside.

2 Place the raspberries in a bowl, add the jam and gently stir so that all the raspberries are coated. Slice the bottom off each apple so that it can sit up straight, then remove the core and seeds (using either a sharp knife or an apple corer).

3 Place the apples on a lipped baking tray or in an ovenproof dish and fill the hole in the centre of each one with the raspberry mixture. Pour the elderflower cordial around the apples and add the butter.

4 Place a pastry hat on top of each apple, brush it with beaten egg, and decorate with your pastry leaves and stalks, sticking them on with beaten egg. Brush again with egg, then generously sprinkle with caster sugar.

5 Bake for 30–35 minutes or until the pastry is golden and crisp and the apples are soft and steaming. Serve each apple with a spoonful of the sticky red glaze and scoops of vanilla ice cream.

mochaccino
TARTS

My favourite way to finish a meal is with good coffee and some rich dark chocolate. These satisfy both.

MAKES
6
TARTS

EQUIPMENT
6 x 10cm round fluted tartlet tins

1 quantity of Chocolate Shortcrust Pastry
  (see page 215)
A little plain flour, for dusting
4 medium egg yolks, lightly beaten
50g golden caster sugar
150g dark chocolate (at least 70% cocoa solids),
  broken up, plus extra for shavings to decorate
150ml espresso or strong coffee, cooled
50ml coffee liqueur, such as Kahlua
200ml double cream

TO DECORATE
400ml double cream
3 tbsp icing sugar

1 Make the chocolate shortcrust pastry according to the method on page 215 and put it into the fridge to rest for 30 minutes.

2 On a lightly floured work surface, roll out the pastry to about 2mm thick. Cut out six 15cm circles and line the tartlet tins with them. Prick the bases with a fork and chill in the fridge for 30 minutes.

3 Preheat the oven to 200°C/fan 180°C/gas mark 6 and put a baking sheet in to heat up. Remove your pastry cases from the fridge, line with crumpled non-stick baking paper and fill with baking beans (see page 211). Bake on the hot baking sheet for 15 minutes, then remove the paper and beans and return to the oven for 5–8 minutes or until the pastry is dry and completely cooked through. Remove the pastry cases from the tins and set aside to cool completely.

4 Beat the egg yolks and caster sugar in a large bowl. Put the chocolate, espresso, coffee liqueur and cream into a separate bowl and stand it over a pan of barely simmering water until melted. Gradually pour the chocolate mixture into the egg mixture, whisking until well mixed, then transfer everything to a clean pan.

5 Place over a gentle heat, stirring constantly with a wooden spoon until the mixture thickens to form a custard. Remove from the heat and pour through a sieve into a jug. Now carefully pour into the pastry cases and place them in the fridge for a minimum of 2 hours to set.

6 To decorate, whip the cream and icing sugar to soft peaks and spoon on top of the tarts, creating a nice swirl with the back of your spoon. Decorate with chocolate shavings.

mini brown sugar
BANOFFEES

MAKES
15–20

EQUIPMENT
2 x shallow bun tins or
1 x mini muffin tray

FOR THE PASTRY
100g unsalted butter, softened
100g soft light brown sugar
2 medium eggs, beaten
325g plain flour, sifted, plus a little for dusting

TO ASSEMBLE
300g condensed caramel (sometimes called
    dulce de leche, available in tins)
300ml extra-thick double cream or lightly
    whipped cream
1–2 ripe bananas, sliced
A little milk chocolate, for shaving
Cocoa powder, for dusting

These miniature banoffee pies are sweet, crunchy and very, very delicious. We like to serve them after dinner, with coffee.

1 Here we like to use little bun tins that produce tarts about 2–3 bites in size. Cut out circles of non-stick baking paper to a size that will fit snugly into the bottom of your tins. Set aside.

2 To make the pastry, beat the butter and brown sugar using an electric whisk until pale (about 5 minutes), then slowly beat in the eggs. Add the flour and beat until just combined, then turn out on to a lightly floured work surface, form into a disc, wrap in clingfilm and chill for at least 30 minutes. Don't be tempted to use it sooner, as this pastry needs to rest.

3 When it's rested, roll out your pastry on a lightly floured work surface to about 2mm thick. Cut or stamp out circles to fit the bun tins or muffin tray, and line the holes with them (don't add the paper circles just yet). Chill for 30 minutes.

4 Preheat the oven to 180°C/fan 160°C/gas mark 4. Line each pastry case with a circle of crumpled non-stick baking paper and fill with baking beans (see page 211). Bake for 10 minutes, then remove the paper and beans and bake for another 5–7 minutes or until crisp. Remove the pastry cases from the tins and allow to cool completely.

5 Now simply assemble the pies. Fill each pastry case with condensed caramel and top with a little dollop of cream, a banana slice, shavings of chocolate and a light dusting of cocoa powder. Beautiful.

lemon posset
TARTS

MAKES
6
TARTS

EQUIPMENT
6 x 10cm shallow round tartlet tins

1 quantity of Sweet Shortcrust Pastry
  (see page 215)
A little plain flour, for dusting
300ml double cream
75g caster sugar
Finely grated zest of 1 lemon
2 tbsp lemon juice
100g fresh raspberries
1–2 tbsp chopped pistachios

I was taught to make lemon posset years ago by a chef who took particular pride in teaching traditional English puddings. He described posset as a luxurious recipe, and when you take a bite I think you'll agree. Instead of traditional ramekins, I've put the posset in buttery pastry cases and added fresh raspberries and chopped pistachios for extra luxuriousness.

1 Make the sweet shortcrust pastry according to the method on page 215 and put it in the fridge to rest for 30 minutes.

2 On a lightly floured work surface, roll out the pastry to about 2mm thick. Cut out six 15cm circles and line your tartlet tins with them. Prick the base of the pastry with a fork, then chill for 30 minutes.

3 Preheat the oven to 200°C/fan 180°C/gas mark 6 and put a baking sheet in to heat up. Line the tartlets with crumpled non-stick baking paper and fill with baking beans (see page 211). Bake on the hot baking sheet in the oven for 15 minutes, then remove the paper and beans and return to the oven for 8–10 minutes or until the edges are turning golden and the pastry is dry to the touch. Set aside to cool completely.

4 Put the cream, sugar and lemon zest into a small pan and place over a low heat, stirring constantly, until the sugar has completely dissolved. When bubbles start to form around the edges of the mixture, continue cooking gently without stirring for 2 minutes, but don't let the mixture boil. Remove from the heat and stir in the lemon juice. Finally, strain into a jug.

5 Remove the cooled tart cases from the tins. Place some raspberries in each one and pour the cooled (but not cold) lemon filling around them, letting some of the fruit poke out. Scatter with the chopped pistachios and put in the fridge for a minimum of 2 hours to set.

TIP

Assemble these no earlier than the morning of the day they are to be eaten. This ensures that the pastry doesn't have a chance to soften and keeps the whole tart deliciously crisp.

HEARTS
full of fruit

Over the years these almondy hearts have been the answer to our search for a frugal, make-ahead pudding that looks completely beautiful. They can be pulled together almost entirely from the storecupboard, using a pack of puff pastry, some marzipan and any fruit you have in the bowl.

EQUIPMENT

1 x 12cm and 1 x 9cm heart-shaped cutter (or make your own templates – see tip, below)

375g all-butter puff pastry

A little plain flour, for dusting

1 medium egg yolk, lightly beaten

Icing sugar, for dusting

175g white marzipan

A small selection of fruit, e.g. berries, freshly sliced nectarines, peeled and sliced eating apples

25g butter, melted

3 tbsp caster sugar

1 On a lightly floured work surface, roll out the puff pastry to 5–6mm thick. Using your larger cutter or template, cut out six heart shapes. Place on a baking sheet lined with non-stick baking paper and brush each one with beaten egg yolk.

2 Preheat the oven to 200°C/fan 180°C/gas mark 6. Dust your work surface with icing sugar and roll out the marzipan to about 4mm thick. Cut out six hearts, using the smaller cutter or template. Place your marzipan hearts on top of the pastry.

3 Arrange a handful of berries or sliced fruit on each marzipan heart. Brush the fruit with melted butter and sprinkle with the caster sugar.

4 Bake in the oven for 15–20 minutes or until the pastry is golden and the fruit has begun to caramelise. Serve warm.

TIP

To make your own templates, use thin cardboard such as an empty cereal packet. Draw a heart shape 12cm across at its widest point and the same lengthways. Alongside it, draw a second heart shape, 1.5cm smaller all round than the first one (therefore 9cm across at its widest point). Cut out both shapes.

easy
EXTRAS
&
proper
PASTRY

sticky
ONIONS

Here, the humble onion is transformed into a sweet, caramelised side dish that makes an unusual but gorgeous accompaniment to our Beef Bourguignon Pie (page 51) or your Sunday roast.

SERVES 4 — AS A SIDE DISH

EQUIPMENT
4 x 10cm round tartlet tins

2 onions, about 150g each
80g caster sugar
A few sprigs of fresh thyme, leaves stripped
A little olive oil
A little plain flour, for dusting
200g all-butter puff pastry
Salt and freshly ground black pepper

1 Preheat the oven to 220°C/fan 200°C/gas mark 7. Prepare your tins by putting a small circle of non-stick baking paper in the base of each.

2 Peel the onions and slice in half, horizontally. Heat the sugar and 80ml water in a small pan over a medium heat, without stirring, until the sugar completely dissolves. Turn up the heat, boil until the syrup turns golden, then immediately pour it into the lined tins – the syrup will solidify very quickly so immediately sprinkle in the thyme leaves and place an onion half, cut side down, into each tin. Season with salt and pepper and brush with a little olive oil.

3 Place the tins on a baking tray and bake for 25 minutes. Remove and allow to cool completely in the tins (leave the oven switched on).

4 Meanwhile, on a lightly floured work surface, roll out the puff pastry to about 3mm thick and cut out four circles, just larger than your tins. Drape the pastry circles over the cooled onions and prick once or twice with a fork. Return to the hot oven for 20 minutes or until the pastry is golden brown.

5 Remove from the oven and, working quickly, carefully turn the tins over on to a baking tray. Remove the tins and serve the onions with a little extra seasoning.

TIP

To clean the caramel from your pan, simply fill with cold water and return to the heat. Bring to the boil and simmer for a few minutes. This makes the residue much easier to tackle!

lemony baby
POTATOES

SERVES 6 AS A SIDE DISH

Glorious new potatoes, lemon and crème fraîche add a touch of luxury to summer suppers. We suggest pairing with our Smoked Salmon and Rocket Tarts (page 134).

1kg baby new potatoes
4 tsp lemon juice
1 tsp Dijon mustard
2 tbsp olive oil
4 tbsp crème fraîche
6 spring onions, finely sliced
6 small cornichons, finely chopped
1 small bunch each of fresh flat-leaf parsley
   and dill, leaves chopped
Salt and freshly ground black pepper

1 Put the potatoes into a large pan of salted water, bring to the boil, then reduce the heat and simmer for 15 minutes or until tender. Drain and transfer to a large bowl.

2 Meanwhile, pour 2 teaspoons of the lemon juice into a small jam jar, add the mustard and oil, and season with salt and pepper. Put the lid on securely and give it a really good shake.

3 Stir the dressing into the warm potatoes and leave to cool for about 30 minutes so that the dressing can be absorbed. Add the crème fraîche, spring onions, cornichons, herbs and remaining lemon juice. Check the seasoning and serve.

spiced
ROASTIES

SERVES 6 AS A SIDE DISH

There's nothing quite like a roast potato to add some welcome crunch to your Sunday lunch. We like to serve these with the No-nonsense Steak and Ale Pie (page 47) – the touch of spice makes the whole meal sparkle.

1kg baby new potatoes
1 tsp coriander seeds, crushed
1 tsp cumin seeds, crushed
3 tbsp olive oil
1 tbsp grainy mustard
1 small bunch of fresh flat-leaf parsley,
   leaves chopped
Salt

1 Preheat the oven to 220°C/fan 200°C/gas mark 7. Bring a large pan of salted water to the boil. Add the potatoes and cook for 15 minutes or until tender. Drain well.

2 Tip the potatoes into a shallow roasting tin and crush them slightly with the back of a fork so that the skins just burst. Sprinkle with the coriander and cumin, drizzle over the oil and season with salt. Roast in the oven for 30 minutes or until crisp and golden. While they're still hot, add the mustard and parsley, and toss to coat.

rich onion
GRAVY

A knob of butter

1 tbsp olive oil

1 large onion, sliced

2 tsp plain flour

75ml white wine

500ml good-quality hot vegetable stock

1 tsp redcurrant jelly

Salt and freshly ground black pepper

Not many sauces have a jug named after them; but such is the importance of gravy! We've used onion and a touch of redcurrant jelly to make this one extra-special.

1 Melt the butter and olive oil in a medium saucepan over a medium-low heat. Cook the onion, stirring occasionally (to stop it catching), for 15–20 minutes or until soft, golden and starting to caramelise.

2 Sprinkle in the flour, stir and cook for 1 minute. Pour in the white wine, allow to bubble until reduced and sticky, then add the stock. Bring to the boil, simmer for 10 minutes, then add the redcurrant jelly and stir to dissolve. Check the seasoning and add salt and pepper to taste. Serve piping hot.

petits pois and
PANCETTA

SERVES
4
AS A
SIDE DISH

A slosh of olive oil

350g cubed pancetta

300g frozen petits pois

¼ of a Savoy cabbage, tough outer leaves discarded and the rest finely shredded

A large knob of butter

A little freshly grated nutmeg

Salt and freshly ground black pepper

Combining peas, one of the sweetest vegetables, with salty pancetta creates a satisfying side dish full of flavour. We think this is best served with any of our chicken pie recipes or a good old lamb Hotpot (see page 26).

1 Heat a slosh of oil in a large shallow pan over a high heat, then add the pancetta and sizzle for a few minutes or until beginning to turn golden. Add the petits pois, cabbage and a splash of water. Cover with a tightly fitting lid and cook over a medium heat for about 3 minutes.

2 Uncover the pan, add the butter, and season with salt, pepper and nutmeg. Serve immediately.

thrifty bubble and squeak CAKES

MAKES
12
CAKES

This classic combination is a great way to use up the extra mash that's left over from your pie toppings. The cakes can be tarted up with a soft poached egg or rasher of crispy bacon on top.

100g cavolo nero, spring greens, Savoy cabbage
 or kale, leaves shredded
600g cold mashed potato (see page 25 for method)
5 spring onions, white and green parts thinly sliced
70g feta cheese, crumbled
A little plain flour, for dusting
A large knob of butter
Salt and freshly ground black pepper

1 Bring a large saucepan of salted water to the boil. Add the shredded greens and cook for 3 minutes or until tender, then drain and run under cold water to stop the cooking. Drain again, then dry the greens on kitchen paper.

2 Put your cold mash into a large bowl. Mix in the blanched greens, spring onions and feta, and season with salt and pepper to taste. Shape into 12 cakes (each about 1cm thick) and dust with a little flour.

3 Melt the butter in a large non-stick frying pan and fry the cakes over a medium heat for 2–3 minutes on each side or until golden and cooked through. Serve warm as a side dish, or topped with a poached egg for lunch.

braised fennel and baby LEEKS

SERVES
6

AS A
SIDE DISH

This is a delicate, pretty side dish that sits particularly nicely with our Hot-smoked Salmon Gougère (page 92).

2 fennel bulbs, trimmed
40g butter
100ml white wine
110g baby leeks
20g Parmesan cheese, finely grated
Salt and freshly ground black pepper

1 Preheat the oven to 180°C/fan 160°C/gas mark 4. Cut the fennel bulbs into thick wedges, keeping the core intact.

2 Melt the butter in a shallow ovenproof pan on a medium heat. Place the fennel cut-side down in the butter. Season with salt and pepper and pour in the white wine. When bubbling, cover tightly with a lid or foil and bake in the oven for 30 minutes.

3 Remove from the oven, turn over the fennel bulbs and add the leeks. Put the lid back on and return to the oven for another 30 minutes or until really tender. Serve sprinkled with the Parmesan and a little more freshly ground black pepper.

garlicky green BEANS

SERVES
6

AS A
SIDE DISH

Green beans are too often cooked for a minute too many! Keep them bright green and crunchy to freshen up any plate. Serve with our Chinese Spiced Beef Pies (page 38).

280g green beans, tops trimmed, tails left on
40g butter
2 large garlic cloves, finely chopped
1 small red chilli, deseeded and finely chopped (optional)
4 spring onions, finely chopped
Salt and freshly ground black pepper

1 Bring a small pan of salted water to the boil. Add the beans and boil for 3 minutes or until just tender, then drain well.

2 Melt the butter in a frying pan. Add the garlic and chilli (if using), fry for 30 seconds, then add the beans and toss to coat in the butter. Cook for a couple of minutes, then toss in the spring onions, give it all a good shake in the pan, and tip into a warm serving bowl. Season with salt and pepper.

spiced apple and onion **CHUTNEY**

MAKES
2X
250 ML
JARS

450g eating apples (6 small apples)

75g raisins or sultanas

1 small onion, finely chopped

160g demerara sugar

½ tsp coriander seeds, crushed

½ tsp smoked paprika

1 cinnamon stick

200ml cider vinegar

Salt

A jar or two of homemade chutney will have you feeling very domestic and is bound to impress guests. It's perfect served with warm, gooey wedges of our Giant Gruyère and Ham Sandwich (page 48).

1 Peel, core and chop the apples and place in a large saucepan with the raisins or sultanas, the onion, sugar and spices.

2 Add the cider vinegar, season generously with salt, and place over a low heat, stirring, until the sugar has dissolved. Cook for 45 minutes, stirring now and then. Cover with a lid halfway through the cooking time.

3 When ready, the chutney will have become thicker and the flavour will have mellowed. You should be able to draw your spoon through the middle and briefly see the base of the pan. Transfer the chutney into sterilised jars, seal and leave to cool. It keeps for about 3 months in the fridge.

fresh red **SALSA**

SERVES
4–6   AS A
SIDE DISH

300g cherry tomatoes, halved

1 large ripe avocado, peeled and stone removed, roughly chopped

½ a red onion, finely chopped

1 green chilli, deseeded and finely diced

1 small bunch of fresh coriander, leaves chopped

Grated zest and juice of ½ a lime

½ tsp caster sugar

A generous glug of extra-virgin olive oil

Salt and freshly ground black pepper

Not only is a fresh salsa very simple and swift to put together, it adds a certain vigour to other recipes. Dollop plenty on top of our Chilli Beef Pie (page 45) to lend a refreshing, zesty kick.

1 Toss the cherry tomato halves and avocado pieces together in a large bowl. Add all the remaining ingredients and give everything a good stir.

2 Set aside for 10 minutes for the flavours to mingle, then check the seasoning and serve. This can be kept in the fridge for up to 24 hours (though the avocado may begin to go brown).

spicy chorizo
<u>BEANS</u>

**SERVES
6**

AS A
SIDE DISH

**These beans are just as good on their own for breakfast
as they are piled next to a grilled chicken breast for supper.
Comfort food with a kick.**

1 tbsp olive oil

1 onion, finely chopped

100g chorizo cooking sausage, chopped

1 large garlic clove, finely chopped

½ tsp dried chilli flakes

400g tin of chopped tomatoes

1 tbsp treacle

1 tsp cider vinegar

1 x 400g tin of haricot or cannellini beans,
    drained and rinsed

Salt and freshly ground black pepper

1 Heat the oil in a large, shallow pan over a medium heat and add
the onion. Cook for 5 minutes to soften, then add the chorizo and cook
for a further 5 minutes. Add the garlic and chilli flakes and cook for
1 minute more.

2 Tip in the tomatoes, treacle, vinegar and 250ml water. Season well
with salt and pepper, bring to a gentle bubble, and cook on a medium-
low heat for 20 minutes, uncovered, until thickened.

3 Now add the beans and cook for another 15 minutes. Check the
seasoning, adjust if necessary and serve warm.

fresh basil
PESTO

MAKES
250
ML

1 garlic clove
2 tbsp pine nuts, toasted
60g fresh basil leaves
20g Parmesan cheese, finely grated
Juice of ½ a lemon
120ml extra-virgin olive oil
Salt and freshly ground black pepper

It is not just Italians who are passionate about pesto. Stir through pasta, add to a dressing or pop a jar of it on the table, alongside the mustard, to complement a warm chicken pie or steaming sausage roll.

1 In the small bowl of a food processor, or using a pestle and mortar, whizz or pound the garlic clove with a pinch of salt. Add the toasted pine nuts and coarsely grind. Then add the basil leaves and keep pounding to a textured paste.

2 Transfer to a bowl and stir in all the remaining ingredients. Check the seasoning, adding more salt and pepper to taste. This keeps for up to a week, covered, in the fridge.

raw cabbage
SLAW

**SERVES
6**   AS A
SIDE DISH

4 rashers of rindless streaky bacon, cut into lardons
¼ of a red cabbage
¼ of a white cabbage
1 small red onion, very finely sliced
1 red-skinned apple, cored and finely sliced
35g pecan nuts, roughly chopped
Mixed fresh herbs, chopped, e.g. mint, dill,
   flat-leaf parsley

Cabbage has long been the victim of bad press, often dismissed as soggy and bland. But this recipe bucks the trend. It's fresh and crisp, with a tart, creamy dressing. Try it alongside our Sausage and Bean Pie (page 15).

1 Fry the bacon in a dry frying pan on a medium-high heat until crisp. Quarter, core and finely shred the red and white cabbage. Put into a large bowl with the red onion, apple, cooked bacon and pecan nuts.

2 For the dressing, whisk together 6 tablespoons of crème fraîche with 2 teaspoons of Dijon mustard and 1 tablespoon each of lemon juice and extra-virgin olive oil, seasoning with salt and pepper to taste. Pour the dressing into the bowl with the cabbage mixture, add the herbs and toss to coat. Serve immediately.

spiced tomato
SAUCE

MAKES
ABOUT
600
ML

Homemade tomato sauce is a great all-rounder, which can always be put to good use. It's a key ingredient in many of the pie fillings throughout this book, and can also be used on pizza or simply stirred through pasta.

2 tbsp olive oil
2 red onions, chopped
2 large garlic cloves, chopped
½ tsp fennel seeds
1 tsp cumin seeds
2 tsp ground coriander
2 x 400g tins of chopped tomatoes
A pinch of salt
1 tbsp soft brown sugar

1 Heat the olive oil in a large shallow pan over a gentle heat. Add the onions and cook them for 5 minutes to soften. Add the garlic and spices to the pan, and cook, stirring, for a couple more minutes.

2 Pour over the tomatoes and add the salt and sugar. Stir well, then simmer gently, uncovered, for about 30 minutes or until slightly syrupy in consistency. The sauce can be kept, covered, in the fridge for up to a week.

puff pastry
CROUTONS

MAKES
ABOUT
24

The ultimate in kitchen recycling – leftover pastry and leftover cheese baked together to create something wonderful that will perk up salads and soups in seconds.

A little plain flour, for dusting
200g all-butter puff pastry
30g Parmesan cheese, finely grated
1 medium egg, lightly beaten

1 Preheat the oven to 220°C/fan 200°C/gas mark 7. On a lightly floured work surface, roll out the pastry to about 4mm thick. Sprinkle half the Parmesan over one half of the pastry, then fold the other half over the top to enclose the cheese. Roll out the pastry again. Brush the top with beaten egg and sprinkle with the remaining Parmesan.

2 Cut into 2cm squares (or stamp out little heart shapes) and place on a baking sheet lined with non-stick baking paper. Bake for 12–15 minutes or until crisp and golden. Toss into a salad or scatter over bowls of steaming soup. These will keep for up to a week in an airtight container.

CAULIFLOWER cheese
with brown sugar onions

Here's a dish that often steals the show, even when served alongside meat recipes. For me, it has that thrilling combination of easy to make and glorious to look at. And it tastes delicious. One for the next family gathering, perhaps.

SERVES
6

EQUIPMENT

1 x 1-litre ovenproof dish

FOR THE BROWN SUGAR ONIONS

2 tbsp butter

2 small or medium red onions, thinly sliced

1½ tbsp brown sugar

FOR THE CAULIFLOWER

1 medium cauliflower, leaves removed and
   stalk trimmed

60g Parmesan cheese, grated

200g crème fraîche

1 medium egg yolk

2 tbsp chopped fresh flat-leaf parsley

2 tbsp pumpkin seeds

1 Begin by caramelising the onions, as this can be a long, slow process. Melt the butter in a large frying pan over a medium-low heat. Add the onions, stir gently to coat with the butter and cook gently, checking on them regularly and stirring occasionally for 20 minutes. This is best done slowly to allow the onions to be meltingly soft. Stir through the brown sugar and 2 tablespoons of water and cook the onions for a further 5–10 minutes until soft and brown.

2 While the onions are finishing caramelising, steam the cauliflower for about 20 minutes, turning halfway through. Transfer to the centre of your ovenproof dish.

3 Preheat oven to 180°C/fan 160°C/gas mark 4. Put three-quarters of the Parmesan, the crème fraîche and egg yolk into a bowl and mix well. Pour over the cauliflower to evenly coat. Pile the caramelised onions on top, then scatter over the parsley, pumpkin seeds and remaining Parmesan.

4 Bake on the middle shelf of the oven for 25–30 minutes or until the cauliflower has turned golden and the cheese has almost burnt in places. Serve immediately.

roasted butternut
squash **WEDGES**

SERVES
6

AS A
SIDE DISH

With its buttery flesh and papery skin, squash responds really well to being roasted and the resulting texture is unbeatable. These wedges are good served with our Chicken and Ham Hock Pie (page 23). Roast a little extra and you'll have a gorgeous standby ingredient to throw into a salad or a pitta for tomorrow's lunch.

1 large butternut squash
4 sprigs of fresh rosemary
2–3 tbsp olive oil
1 bulb whole garlic, split into cloves and
    bruised (press with the side of a knife
    to crack the skins)
2 sprigs of fresh oregano, leaves stripped
    and chopped
Salt and freshly ground black pepper

1 Preheat the oven to 220°C/fan 200°C/gas mark 7.

2 Halve the squash and remove the seeds, leaving the skin on, then cut it into wedges (approximately 2cm thick). Scatter over a large shallow ovenproof dish or roasting tin. Add the rosemary sprigs, drizzle with the oil and season with salt and pepper. Toss to coat, then add the bruised garlic to the tin.

3 Roast in the oven for 30–40 minutes until the squash is tender and starting to caramelise. Sprinkle over the oregano and roast for 5 minutes more. Season again and serve.

perfect
PASTRY

Making your own pastry is both rewarding and therapeutic. On the next few pages are recipes for savoury shortcrust pastry plus some variations and twists. Remember, a few important things hold true whatever type of pastry you are making: always measure your ingredients accurately, keep everything as cold as possible and don't be tempted to handle the pastry too much or it can become tough and chewy. Most of all, just have a go and don't panic.

a few tips for handling pastry

Resting your pastry
Once you have made your pastry, it's really important to let it sit in the fridge for at least 30 minutes. This allows the pastry to relax, which helps reduce any shrinking when it's in the oven, as well as making it firmer and easier to roll. Please don't be tempted to bypass this stage.

Rolling, lining and trimming
After your pastry has relaxed in the fridge, allow a further 10 minutes for it to 'warm up' at room temperature before you begin rolling. This also applies to blocks of ready-made pastry bought from the supermarket.

Dust your work surface and rolling pin lightly with flour to prevent the pastry sticking and tearing, then begin to roll it out, rolling away from yourself and in just one direction at a time. The goal is to flatten the pastry rather than stretch it, so turn it frequently – this helps to achieve an even thickness all over. Remember to turn the pastry, not your body! If the pastry sticks to the work surface, loosen by sliding a palette knife underneath.

For really delicate pastries such as sweet ones made with lots of butter and sugar, it's best to roll between sheets of non-stick baking paper.

If your rolled-out pastry is covered in excess flour, lightly flick a dry pastry brush over the top and bottom to remove it. Then gently ease the pastry into the tin or pie dish, taking care not to stretch the pastry.

Once you've lined your tart tin or pie dish, you can roll a rolling pin across the top of the tin to loosen any excess pastry at the sides. Then use a small sharp knife to cut away this excess, working around the sides in sweeping downward strokes, turning the tin as you go. This is easiest if you hold the tin at eye level.

Now gently prick the base of the pastry with a fork. This helps release trapped air so that it stays flat while baking. But try not to prick all the way through the base or your filling may escape later on.

Crimping

Crimping is a method used to seal the pastry around the edge of your pie dish or tin. It also looks lovely, of course. The easiest way to crimp is to pinch the edges of the pastry between your thumb and forefinger, or you can press into the pastry with the prongs of a fork or even the back of a teaspoon. Make sure to pinch or press firmly – anything too subtle will just disappear while baking.

Knocking up

Knocking up is a technique sometimes used for puff pastry – it helps loosen the layers of pastry and let air get in between them, which encourages the pastry to puff up and makes the pie look glorious. To do this, hold the blade of a very sharp knife horizontally to the edge of your raw pastry case and, with your other hand, press down gently on the edge of the pastry next to the knife. Tap gently into the edge of the pastry all the way round the pie, then brush the top of the pie with beaten egg – trying really hard not to let any egg drip down on to the knocked-up sides as it will stop them separating and puffing up.

Decorating and glazing

Decorating the top of your pie with pastry shapes is a great way to use up scraps and give a hint as to what's inside. Gather up your scraps of leftover pastry and roll out to about 2mm thick. Use pastry cutters or go freestyle to make pretty decorations such as leaves, apples, fishes, hearts and stars. Arrange over the top of your pie lid and secure in place with a little beaten egg. If your decorations are especially thick, you might need to add a few extra minutes to the baking time.

At Higgidy, we love to add a heavy glaze, to give our pies a gorgeous golden sheen. Experiment with lightly beaten egg, single cream or whole milk. For a really intense sheen and a rich golden colour, you can double-glaze. It's exactly as it sounds – brush the pie lid with beaten egg and then brush it again. Or for a super-glossy finish, add a single egg yolk to your beaten-egg mixture.

After glazing you can sprinkle the top of your pie with spices, herbs, grated cheese, nuts, seeds or sugar. Our favourite toppings are dried chilli flakes, caraway or black onion seeds, ground polenta, pink peppercorns and golden granulated sugar.

Blind baking

You may have wondered what this term means. Put simply, it's the process of baking an empty pastry case before adding a filling. This is necessary when the pastry takes longer to cook than the filling, so blind baking gives it a headstart. It also helps prevent the pastry becoming soggy once the filling is added.

To blind bake your pastry case, make sure you have pricked the base several times with a fork, then line with a circle of crumpled non-stick baking paper wide enough to come up the sides. Fill with a generous layer of ceramic baking beans, though not so full it's at risk of overflowing. (If you don't have ceramic beans, dried beans or chickpeas work equally well. You can re-use them too – let them cool down completely, then store in a jar.) The beans provide support for the sides and weigh down the empty base so it doesn't rise up while baking. Then bake the pastry case as instructed in the recipe.

If you find a few cracks or holes after the case is baked, don't panic. Just take a bit of leftover raw pastry and patch up the holes, then brush with beaten egg and soldier on! These little bits of raw pastry will bake with the filling.

A note about puff, filo and other types of pastry

You will notice we've not given recipes for making puff pastry or filo pastry from scratch. This is because both are very fiddly and time-consuming to make, so we recommend you use shop-bought. For puff pastry, the all-butter variety tastes the nicest and puffs up beautifully into crisp layers.

A few recipes in this book call for more complicated pastry techniques, such as the Hot-smoked Salmon Gougère on page 92, which involves choux pastry, or the Wonderful Wedding Pie on pages 81–83, which is made with hot-water crust pastry. For these, you'll find detailed instructions in the recipe itself, but the basic principles still apply – measuring carefully, keeping the pastry cold, allowing it time to rest and not over-handling.

savoury
shortcrust <u>PASTRY</u>

**MAKES
350G**

200g plain flour
A generous pinch of salt
100g butter, well chilled and cut into small cubes
30g Parmesan cheese, grated (optional)
1 medium egg yolk, beaten
About 3 tbsp ice-cold water

Traditional shortcrust pastry is made up of two parts plain flour to one part fat (such as butter or lard), plus a tiny amount of cold water. At Higgidy, we've had lots of practice making shortcrust pastry, so here is our trusted recipe, which is both delicious and easy to handle. For the ultimate savoury flavour, we add cheese. This makes it taste great and gives the pastry a gorgeous golden colour when baked, but you can leave this out if you prefer a more traditional approach. To make a richer pastry you can add a touch more butter and an egg yolk, or for a shorter, silkier texture you can use a combination of butter and lard. The pastry can be made easily by hand or in a food processor.

How it's done – by hand
Sift the flour and salt into a large mixing bowl. Add the butter cubes and use your fingertips and thumbs to lightly rub it into the flour until the mixture resembles breadcrumbs. Add the Parmesan (if using) and rub again until the cheese is mixed in evenly. Now add the beaten egg yolk and water, and use a round-bladed knife to combine the wet ingredients with the dry until the pastry comes together. Gather it up with your hands and knead very briefly into a ball on a lightly floured surface. Try not to handle it too much at this stage, or the fat will get warm and the pastry will become tricky to use and may turn out tough and chewy. Wrap in clingfilm and chill for 30 minutes before use.

How it's done – in a food processor
Making shortcrust pastry in a food processor takes just minutes. Process the flour, butter and cheese (if using) until the mixture resembles breadcrumbs. Add the egg yolk beaten with the ice-cold water. Pulse until the mixture just comes together to form a dough, adding a tiny bit more water if you think it's needed. Wrap in clingfilm and chill for 30 minutes.

If you're feeling adventurous…

Once you've mastered the basics of shortcrust pastry you can experiment with the sweet and gluten-free versions overleaf and on page 216, and with adding extra flavours such as nuts, herbs or seeds – see suggestions below. Stir in once the mixture resembles fine breadcrumbs, just before you add the egg yolk and water. Be aware that some additions, such as moist herbs or oily nuts, can make the pastry harder to handle. Try the following:

* A tablespoon of finely chopped fresh herbs – woody herbs such as thyme, rosemary and oregano work best. Avoid wetter herbs like chives or parsley, and remember to remove any stalks before chopping.

* A couple of teaspoons of seeds, such as sesame, poppy, black onion or caraway. These add flavour and texture to the pastry. The darker-coloured seeds look really pretty too.

* Spices, such as a pinch of saffron threads, paprika or chilli flakes. These taste delicious and give the pastry a beautiful colour.

* 40–50g finely chopped walnuts, pecans or hazelnuts. You can add these to both savoury and sweet shortcrust pastry.

* Grated lemon, lime or orange zest, to give sweet shortcrust pastry some zing. Use your finest grater to achieve the best distribution through the pastry, and add the zest to the flour before rubbing in the butter.

sweet shortcrust
PASTRY

**MAKES
500G**

This simple sweetened shortcrust is great for any fresh fruit pie or sweet deep-filled tart. See page 213 for extra ingredients you can add to make it even more delicious.

250g plain flour, plus a little for dusting
50g icing sugar
A pinch of salt
135g butter, well chilled and cut into small cubes
1 medium egg, beaten
2–3 tbsp ice-cold water or whole milk

Sift the flour, icing sugar and salt into a large bowl or a food processor. Add the butter cubes and lightly rub in with your fingertips or pulse until the mixture resembles breadcrumbs. Add the beaten egg and cold water or milk and use a round-bladed knife or pulse to combine the ingredients until the pastry comes together, adding a tiny bit more liquid if needed. Gather it up with your hands and knead very briefly into a ball on a lightly floured surface. Try not to handle it too much at this stage, or the fat will get warm and the pastry will become tricky to use and may turn out tough and chewy. Wrap in clingfilm and chill for 30 minutes before use.

chocolate shortcrust
PASTRY

**MAKES
375G**

It's fun to complement a rich chocolate filling with chocolate pastry. It's also lovely blind-baked and filled with fresh berries and a warm berry jam glaze.

175g plain flour, plus a little for dusting
1 tbsp good-quality cocoa powder
50g icing sugar
100g unsalted butter, chilled and cut into small cubes
1 medium egg yolk, beaten
1–2 tbsp ice-cold water

Sift the flour, cocoa powder and icing sugar into a large bowl or a food processor and rub in or process with the butter until the mixture resembles breadcrumbs. Add the beaten egg yolk and ice-cold water, then stir or pulse just enough to bring the pastry together. Turn out on to a lightly floured work surface and knead lightly until smooth. Try not to handle too much at this stage or the fat will get warm and the pastry may turn out tough and chewy. Wrap in clingfilm and chill for 30 minutes before use.

gluten-free shortcrust
PASTRY

MAKES
400G

150g potato flour, plus a little for dusting

65g fine-ground polenta

1 tsp xanthan gum

A pinch of salt

140g butter, well chilled and cut into small cubes

1 medium egg, beaten

1 tbsp ice-cold water (optional)

Gluten is a protein found in cereals such as wheat, and therefore in most types of flour. When mixed with water it forms stretchy strands that give pastry its consistency and make it suitable for rolling, cutting and lining tins or pie dishes. So the big challenge with gluten-free pastry is in achieving the same consistency as with a wheat-based one. While writing this book we've experimented with different flours and also xanthan gum, a powerful thickening agent that helps make the pastry stretchy. You'll find it in the baking aisle of the supermarket. After lots of trial and error, we think this recipe works pretty well. It's quite delicate so is best made by hand.

1 Put the potato flour, polenta, xanthan gum and salt into a large bowl. Add the butter cubes to the bowl and, using your fingertips and thumbs, lightly rub together until the mixture resembles breadcrumbs.

2 Now add the beaten egg and use a round-bladed knife to combine with the dry ingredients until the pastry comes together. You might need a splash of ice-cold water to bring it together. Using your hands, gather it up and knead very briefly on a surface lightly dusted with potato flour. Form into a ball. Try not to handle it too much at this stage, or the fat will get warm and the pastry will become tricky to use and may turn out tough and chewy. Wrap in clingfilm and chill for 30 minutes before use.

3 Roll and line according to the recipe you are following, but to bake blind (see page 211) with gluten-free pastry, you need to reduce the oven temperature by 10°C (or by one gas mark) and the cooking time by 5 minutes.

quick soured cream **PASTRY**

MAKES
400G

This lovely pastry is super-quick to make and has a very soft texture. As long as you don't over-mix, it's almost foolproof. Try adding fresh herbs, such as thyme or oregano.

175g plain flour, plus a little for dusting
A tiny pinch of salt
150g butter, well chilled and cut into small cubes
90ml soured cream

Sift the flour and salt into a large bowl or food processor and add the butter. Rub in with your fingertips or pulse until the mixture resembles breadcrumbs. Add the soured cream and stir or pulse for 2–3 seconds, or until just mixed. Bring together on a lightly floured surface and shape into a flat disc, then wrap in clingfilm and chill for 30 minutes before use.

savoury croustade **PASTRY**

MAKES
350G

Try making this rich, cheesy pastry for any of our croustades or for a freeform pie. The cheese gives it a lovely nutty brown colour when baked, and it tastes delicious.

200g plain flour, plus a little for dusting
A generous pinch of salt
75g butter, well chilled and cut into small cubes
50g mature Cheddar cheese, finely grated
1 medium egg, beaten
1–2 tbsp ice-cold water

Sift the flour and salt into a large bowl or a food processor, add the butter cubes and rub in with your fingertips or pulse until the mixture resembles breadcrumbs. Add the grated Cheddar, and stir or pulse until the cheese is just mixed in. Add the beaten egg and a few splashes of ice-cold water and mix or pulse just enough to bring the pastry together. Turn out on to a lightly floured work surface and knead lightly until smooth. Try not to handle too much or the fat will get warm and the pastry may turn out tough and chewy. Wrap in clingfilm and chill for 30 minutes before use.

Index

Metric/Imperial Conversion Charts

WEIGHT CONVERSIONS

5 g	1/8 oz
10 g	¼ oz
15 g	½ oz
25/30g	1 oz
35 g	1¼ oz
40 g	1½ oz
50 g	1¾ oz
55 g	2 oz
60 g	2¼ oz
70 g	2½ oz
85 g	3 oz
90 g	3¼ oz
100 g	3½ oz
115 g	4 oz
125 g	4½ oz
140 g	5 oz
150 g	5½ oz
175 g	6 oz
200 g	7 oz
225 g	8 oz
250 g	9 oz
275 g	9¾ oz
280 g	10 oz
300 g	10½ oz
325 g	11½ oz
350 g	12 oz
375 g	13 oz
400 g	14 oz
425 g	15 oz
450 g	1 lb
500 g	1 lb 2 oz
550 g	1 lb 4 oz
600 g	1 lb 5 oz
650 g	1 lb 7 oz
700 g	1 lb 9 oz
750 g	1 lb 10 oz
800 g	1 lb 12 oz

LIQUID CONVERSIONS

1.25 ml	¼ tsp
2.5 ml	½ tsp
5 ml	1 tsp
10 ml	2 tsp
15 ml	1 tbsp / 3 tsp / ½ fl oz
30 ml	2 tbsp / 1 fl oz
45 ml	3 tbsp
50 ml	2 fl oz
60 ml	4 tbsp
75 ml	5 tbsp / 2½ fl oz
90 ml	6 tbsp
100 ml	3½ fl oz
125 ml	4 fl oz
150 ml	5 fl oz / ¼ pt
175 ml	6 fl oz
200 ml	7 fl oz / 1/3 pt
225 ml	8 fl oz
250 ml	9 fl oz
300 ml	10 fl oz / ½ pt
350 ml	12 fl oz
400 ml	14 fl oz
425 ml	15 fl oz / ¾ pt
450 ml	16 fl oz
500 ml	18 fl oz
568 ml	1 pint
600 ml	20 fl oz
700 ml	1¼ pint
850 ml	1½ pint
1 litre	1¾ pint

OVEN TEMPERATURES

150°C	300°F
160°C	325°F
180°C	350°F
190°C	375°F
200°C	400°F
220°C	425°F
230°C	450°F

A note on egg size: For UK readers, eggs should be medium unless otherwise specified, which is the equivalent of a large egg in the US.

Glossary of UK & US Terms

aubergine	eggplant
bacon rasher	bacon piece
baking sheet	cookie sheet
beetroot	beet
bicarbonate of soda	baking soda
Bovril	beef extract; beef base
broad bean	ava bean
caster sugar	superfine sugar
(Swiss) chard	silverbeet
chickpeas	garbanzo beans
choux pastry	cream puff paste
chipolata sausages	cocktail sausage
coley	pollock
coriander, fresh	cilantro
cornflour	cornstarch
courgette	zucchini
cream: double, single/pouring	heavy, light or half and half
dark chocolate	bittersweet chocolate
demerara sugar	light brown sugar
filo pastry	phyllo pastry
flour: plain, self-raising	all-purpose, self-rising
(to) grill, (a) grill	broil, broiler
haricot beans	navy beans
icing sugar	confectioners' sugar
jam	jelly
minced beef/lamb	ground beef/lamb
muscovado sugar	light brown sugar
natural yoghurt	plain yoghurt
pepper	bell pepper
petit pois	baby peas
polenta	cornmeal
rocket	arugula
samphire	sea beans
semi-skimmed milk	2% milk
spring onion	scallion/green onion
sultana	golden raisin
swede	rutabaga
treacle	molasses

An Hachette UK Company
www.hachette.co.uk

First published in Great Britain in 2018
by Mitchell Beazley,
an imprint of
Octopus Publishing Group Ltd
Carmelite House
50 Victoria Embankment
London EC4Y 0DZ
www.octopusbooks.co.uk
www.octopusbooksusa.com

Some of this material was previously published in 2013 by Quercus as *The Higgidy Cookbook*

Distributed in the US by
Hachette Book Group
1290 Avenue of the Americas
4th and 5th Floors
New York, NY 10104

Distributed in Canada by
Canadian Manda Group
664 Annette St.
Toronto, Ontario, Canada M6S 2C8

ISBN 978 1 78472 493 1

A CIP catalogue record for this book is available from the British Library.

Printed and bound in China

10 9 8 7 6 5 4 3 2 1

Group Publishing Director: Denise Bates
Editorial Assistant: Emily Brickell
Art Director: Yasia Williams-Leedham
Senior Production Controller: Allison Gonsalves
Designer: Nicky Collings
Photography: Dan Jones
Food styling: Lucy O'Reilly and Georgina Fuggle
Prop styling: Tamzin Ferdinando and Tonia Shuttleworth